PRAISE FOR JIM

"Jim Cobb is perhaps the most well-respected community."

—Joe Alton, MD, coauthor of *The Survival Medicine Handbook*

"Jim Cobb is one of the most practical, no-nonsense preparedness authors around. You can always count on him to cut through the nonsense of unrealistic advice and boil it down to logical, down-to-earth steps that will work for anyone."

—Daisy Luther, founder of TheOrganicPrepper.com

"Jim Cobb is the voice of reason and experience with all things survival. If he says something works, then you know you're getting solid, field-tested information from a respected leader in the survival industry who is constantly applying his skills and incorporating what he teaches into his daily life."

—Tony Nester, author of *Knife-Only Survival*

"Jim Cobb is a master at what it takes to survive in the city or anywhere. He provides you with the basic skills and knowledge for handling challenging situations ethically, with the big picture in mind. Jim gives you the tools and the knowledge for finding your path of self-reliance, for surviving with a smile when others are panicking."

—Christopher Nyerges, author of *How to Survive Anywhere*

"Jim Cobb has rapidly established himself as one of the leading authorities in the preparedness and survival field. He has shown time and time again that he knows his stuff and, most importantly, knows how to convey that knowledge to his readers."

—Scott B. Williams, author of *Bug Out*, *The Pulse*, and *The Darkness After*

"If ... you're serious about prepping, you should seek out serious advice. That means seeking out the experts who have no particular political or religious dogma to sell, experts who are laser focused on what works. Jim Cobb is one such expert."

—Mike Mullin, author of *Ashfall*, *Ashen Winter*, *Darla's Story*, and *Sunrise*

"In the disaster-preparedness community, most people just talk the talk. Jim Cobb is one of the few who walks the walk!"

—Creek Stewart, author of *Build the Perfect Bug Out Bag*

PRAISE FOR *PREPPER'S HOME DEFENSE*

"Jim does a great job in laying out the options and helping the reader wade through all of the available weapons choices. I especially liked his improvised 'hand spike' fashioned from a hubcap removal tool. ... If you like reading about prepping—especially defense—you will like this book. It's a great compilation of security strategies to help protect your 'fort' and 'family.'"

—Creek Stewart, author of *The Unofficial Hunger Games Wilderness Survival Guide*

"Two things I especially like about the book are that it is realistic and that I couldn't find any really bad advice. ... I feel Cobb tells readers what they should hear, which is a credit to him."

—Charlie Palmer, author of *The Prepper Next Door*

PRAISE FOR *THE PREPPER'S COMPLETE BOOK OF DISASTER READINESS*

"Unlike many of the books in this genre, Jim's does not resort to scare tactics—one of my pet peeves. I highly recommend this book. The information is well researched and just might save your life."

—Arthur T. Bradley, PhD, author of *Prepper's Instruction Manual* and *Handbook to Practical Disaster Preparedness for the Family*

"Jim Cobb has been a 'go-to guy' on the internet for a long time, and I think with this volume, he's collected a canon of survival knowledge and training. The chapters on survivalism in fiction and the survival library section are worth it alone."

—Sean T. Page, author of *The Official Zombie Handbook, War Against the Walking Dead,* and *Zombie Survival Manual*

PREPPER'S LONG-TERM SURVIVAL
COUNTDOWN TO PREPAREDNESS

PREPPER'S LONG-TERM SURVIVAL
COUNTDOWN TO PREPAREDNESS

THE PREPPER'S 52-WEEK COURSE TO TOTAL DISASTER READINESS

JIM COBB

Text copyright © 2014, 2025 Jim Cobb. Design and concept copyright © 2014, 2025 Ulysses Press and its licensors. All rights reserved. Any unauthorized duplication in whole or in part or dissemination of this edition by any means (including but not limited to photocopying, electronic devices, digital versions, and the internet) will be prosecuted to the fullest extent of the law.

Published by:
Ulysses Press
an imprint of The Stable Book Group
32 Court Street, Suite 2109
Brooklyn, NY 11201
www.ulyssespress.com

ISBN: 978-1-56975-001-8
Library of Congress Control Number: 2025930794

Printed in the United States
10 9 8 7 6 5 4 3 2 1

Managing editor: Claire Chun
Editor: Laura Schiffman
Proofreader: Janet Vail
Indexer: S4Carlisle Publishing Services
Front cover design: Jake Flaherty
Production: Abbey Gregory
Artwork from shutterstock.com. Cover: generator © Potashev Aleksandr, food © by-studio, first aid © Aleksey Matrenin, water © zstock, wood © Alena Matrosova; page 9: first aid pack © Aleksey Matrenin, backpack © David Pereiras, cans © by-studio-int; page 49: metal tin © wonderisland, first aid © Kostikova Natalia, garden © lunamarina; page 89: gun © Evgeny Haritonov, pot © agsaz, tools © Neflo Photo; page 125: saw © Serz 72, dishware © Pla2na, map © Triff; page 161: masks © AlphaTravels, generator © joe994, shelter © James Aloysius Mahan V

NOTE TO READERS: This book is independently authored and published and no sponsorship or endorsement of this book by, and no affiliation with, any trademarked product mentioned or pictured within is claimed or suggested. All trademarks that appear in the text, illustrations, or photographs in this book belong to their respective owners and are used here for informational purposes only. The author and publisher encourage readers to patronize the recommended products mentioned and pictured in this book. This book has been written and published strictly for informational purposes, and in no way should be used as a substitute for actual instruction with qualified professionals. The author and publisher are providing you with information in this work so that you can have the knowledge and can choose, at your own risk, to act on that knowledge. The author and publisher also urge all readers to be aware of their health status, to consult local fish and game laws, and to consult health care and outdoor professionals before engaging in any potentially hazardous activity. Any use of the information in this book is made on the reader's good judgment. The author and publisher assume no liability for personal injury to the reader or others harmed by the reader, property damage, consequential damage or loss, however caused, from using the information in this book.

*To my beautiful granddaughter Ollie:
You bring us such joy and laughter, and we can't wait until
you're old enough to go camping with grandma and I.*

CONTENTS

Foreword. xi
Introduction 1
How to Use This Book. 5

SECTION I: THE BASICS. 9
- ❏ **Week 1:** Lists, Lists, and More Lists 10
- ❏ **Week 2:** Out with the Old. 15
- ❏ **Week 3:** Basic Water Storage 18
- ❏ **Week 4:** Financial Preps 23
- ❏ **Week 5:** Bug Out Bags .28
- ❏ **Week 6:** Talking to Your Immediate Family About Prepping. 32
- ❏ **Week 7:** PACE Planning 35
- ❏ **Week 8:** Special Prep Considerations: Children 38
- ❏ **Week 9:** Special Prep Considerations: Pets 42
- ❏ **Week 10:** Basic Food Storage 46

SECTION II: SPRING 49
- ❏ **Week 11:** Water Filtration and Purification 50
- ❏ **Week 12:** Planning Your Garden 55
- ❏ **Week 13:** Basic First Aid Supplies and Training 59
- ❏ **Week 14:** Communications: Two-Way Radios and Cell Phones. 64

- ❏ Week 15: Human Waste Disposal 67
- ❏ Week 16: Keeping Clean 70
- ❏ Week 17: Over-the-Counter and Prescription
  Medications 73
- ❏ Week 18: Staying on Top of Medical and
  Dental Issues 76
- ❏ Week 19: Networking 79
- ❏ Week 20: Making Fire 82
- ❏ Week 21: Entertainment 85

SECTION III: SUMMER 89
- ❏ Week 22: Firearms 90
- ❏ Week 23: Alternate Modes of Transportation 93
- ❏ Week 24: Preparing Food Off-Grid 96
- ❏ Week 25: Hidden Storage 100
- ❏ Week 26: Hand Tools 103
- ❏ Week 27: Sugar, Spice, and Everything Nice 107
- ❏ Week 28: Improvised Weapons 111
- ❏ Week 29: Ham Radio 114
- ❏ Week 30: Safety Equipment 117
- ❏ Week 31: Blades for Survival 121

SECTION IV: FALL 125
- ❏ Week 32: Everyday Carry 126
- ❏ Week 33: Mass-Casualty Events 130
- ❏ Week 34: Planning to Regroup 134
- ❏ Week 35: Nonfood Pantry Items 137
- ❏ Week 36: Crank Radios and Police Scanners 140
- ❏ Week 37: Site Security Survey 143
- ❏ Week 38: Structure Hardening Part I:
  Doors and Windows 146
- ❏ Week 39: Structure Hardening Part II: Alarms 150
- ❏ Week 40: Reducing Your Footprint 153
- ❏ Week 41: Practicing Situational Awareness 156

SECTION V: WINTER 161

- ❏ **Week 42**: Planning for Postcollapse Excursions 162
- ❏ **Week 43**: Odds and Ends to Stock Up On 166
- ❏ **Week 44**: Vehicle Emergency Kits 169
- ❏ **Week 45**: The Death File 173
- ❏ **Week 46**: Building Microclimates 177
- ❏ **Week 47**: Bulking Up the Pantry 181
- ❏ **Week 48**: Inventory: The Basics 184
- ❏ **Week 49**: The Survival and Preparedness Library 187
- ❏ **Week 50**: Emergency Lighting 193
- ❏ **Week 51**: Drills, Drills, and More Drills 196
- ❏ **Week 52**: Electrical Power 199

How Did You Do? 203

One Final Lesson: When Normalcy Returns 206

Index 208

Acknowledgments 216

About the Author 217

FOREWORD

In a world where unpredictability is now the norm, preparedness is no longer just a skill—it's a way of life. When Jim Cobb first wrote *Countdown to Preparedness*, he gave us more than just a book; he offered a road map to self-reliance, resilience, and security. I've had the pleasure of knowing and working with Jim and following his work for years. His dedication to helping individuals and families become self-sufficient has made him one of the most respected voices in survival and preparedness today.

What sets Jim apart is his no-nonsense approach to readiness. He understands that preparedness doesn't have to be overwhelming or reserved for extreme scenarios. Instead, he breaks it down into actionable steps that anyone can follow, whether you're new to the world of preparedness or a seasoned expert. In this second edition of *Countdown to Preparedness*, Jim takes you through a clear week-by-week plan to equip you with skills, resources, and knowledge to face the unexpected with confidence.

Jim's insights are grounded in practicality, a quality that resonates deeply with my own experience as an instructor and author. Like Jim, I believe that anyone—regardless of their background—can and should learn the basics of self-reliance. Preparedness is about empowering ourselves and protecting those we care about, and this book embodies that spirit.

As you begin this journey through *Countdown to Preparedness*, know that you're in capable hands. Jim's advice is grounded in real-world experience, tested strategies, and a passion for helping people. His expertise, presented in these pages, will prepare you for potential disruptions and build a mindset of resilience that extends far beyond the scenarios in this book.

I hope this book is a practical and inspiring guide to a more prepared and resilient life. It's an honor to contribute to this work and to support Jim's mission of helping others in their journey toward self-reliance.

—Craig Caudill
Director of Nature Reliance School,
author, instructor, and professional in
preparedness and survival training

INTRODUCTION

Back in late October 2011, the hype about the dreaded "Mayan prophecy" surrounding 12/21/2012 was in full swing. Although I wasn't worried about these dire predictions, I did see them as an opportunity to get more people actively involved with prepping. The Countdown to Preparedness was born in December 2011 on SurvivalWeekly.com. I posted one lesson, complete with assignments, every week for the next year. I had it timed so the final lesson would post just before the predicted end of the world in December 2012.

While I'd hoped the project would garner a bit of interest, I was astounded at how popular it became. I fielded many emails and messages from readers who were loving the weekly lesson format. I got to hear how some folks had used these lessons to ease into prepping, which made things much easier with their less interested spouses. As time went on, more and more people seemed to be following the project. When we finally reached the end, I can't say who was more disappointed, the readers or me. The whole project was truly a lot of fun.

Even before the final lesson was posted, I had people asking me if I was going to turn the online project into a book. I'd been thinking the same thing but was, at the time, eyeball-deep into final edits on my first book, *Prepper's Home Defense*, and starting my second book, *The Prepper's Complete Book of Disaster Readiness*. So while the idea interested me, I had to push it aside to work on other commitments.

As I tackled my various book projects and other endeavors, I noticed a few books coming out, mostly self-published but some from traditional publishers, that had a similar theme, that of getting prepared within a certain time frame. Often, it was thirty days, or four weeks, or some other ridiculously short length of time. Unless you've already done most of the work ahead of time, there's no way you could reach any real degree of preparedness in a month. That's sort of like saying you could take a couch potato and have him or her win the Boston Marathon after a few weeks of training. I suppose if one has an unlimited budget and twelve free hours every day, one might be disaster ready in a month . . . maybe.

Being better prepared isn't, or at least shouldn't be, just about buying stuff. Skills trump stuff every single time. The skills one needs to learn are vast and varied, from first aid to starting campfires, from weapon use and maintenance to food preservation. These aren't things that can be learned overnight. It takes time, it takes energy, and, yes, it does take some money.

Finally, early in 2013, my awesome editor at Ulysses Press, Keith Riegert, and I talked about the Countdown project. At the time, I was working my way through my third book with Ulysses, *Prepper's Long-Term Survival Guide*. I told Keith that I wanted to do Countdown as a book and that if we were going to do it, we should do it sooner rather than later.

The first edition of *Countdown to Preparedness* was released in 2014. It quickly gained a following as readers embraced the "slow and steady wins the race" approach to prepping. By breaking such a huge topic into bite-size chunks, people didn't feel intimidated.

Over the years, I heard from many people who had followed the curriculum and found it helpful. I even fielded messages from a few who had used the material as a textbook to teach others.

As we were wrapping up the revisions for the second edition of *Prepper's Long-Term Survival Guide*, I brought up the idea of revising *Countdown to Preparedness* as well. After all, it'd been about a decade, and during that time, I'd thought of other topics I'd wished I'd included in the book. The folks at Ulysses Press thought it was a great idea, so I went to work.

We kept the same format but swapped out several lessons for what I feel are even more relevant and important topics. I also went through every single page to check for information that needed to be updated. Along the way, I added a fair bit of content to many of the lessons.

The basic idea behind the project hasn't changed. If you follow each lesson and complete all the assignments, by the time you're done, you'll be about as prepared as you can possibly be for any reasonably expected disaster scenario. With that in mind, don't expect this to be all fun and games. There's going to be a lot of hard work ahead, as well as some expense. Many of us preppers and survivalists have been at this for a long time now. If you're brand-new to this whole thing, you have some catching up to do. But if you take it week by week, you'll do just fine.

Now, quiet down. Class is about to begin.

HOW TO USE THIS BOOK

Unlike most books you've read, this one isn't designed to go cover to cover in page order. While you could certainly go that route, doing so will detract from the learning process.

You'll notice the first section is titled "The Basics." No matter where you are in your prepping journey, no matter what time of year it may be as you're reading this, do the lessons in "The Basics" first. They lay the groundwork for many of the future lessons.

Once you've finished the first ten lessons and assignments, move to the section that corresponds to the current season. You're welcome to skip around the book, if that's your preference, but some of the lessons are rather seasonal. For example, it makes little sense to plan out your garden in late summer.

Each week will bring you a lesson to be read, absorbed, and incorporated into your disaster readiness plans. This lesson is followed by a short series of assignments.

I suggest that you pick a day of the week, say Sunday, and commit to visiting this book every week on that day. Have a notebook next to you so you can jot down notes for what you need to do that week. Don't be afraid to dog-ear pages, use a highlighter on the text, or make notes in the margins. By the time you've finished the book, if it looks beat to hell, then you did it right!

ASSIGNMENTS

TASKS

Each lesson includes one or more tasks to be completed. These tasks relate directly to the lesson. Some tasks require nothing more than a pen and paper, while others involve some work and/or expense.

SAVINGS

Each week, you'll be asked to set aside a certain amount of money in what I call the Prepper Savings Account. There will be a few higher-priced items you'll be asked to purchase. Setting aside a little money each week will help you acquire those things when the time comes. If you can't afford to set aside the suggested amount in a particular week, just do what you can and try to make up the difference later. It would be best if you set aside this money as cash, rather than sitting in a bank. Cash will give you the ability to make purchases as needed at rummage sales and such without needing to hit an ATM first.

WATER STORAGE

Water is a key element of any survival plan. Each week, you'll be asked to store a certain quantity of water. While the amounts are small each week, they add up quickly.

GROCERY LIST

Each week, you'll also be asked to purchase a few food items. Occasionally, they will be nonedible supplies. These purchases are in addition to anything else you'd buy that week for your overall disaster plans. On average, you should expect to pay under $20 for the groceries specified each week.

BUYING IN BULK

Shopping at a warehouse store will often stretch your buying dollar. But it comes at the cost of sometimes having to lay out a substantial amount of money at one time. Many people just don't have the funds to spend on case lots of canned goods and other items. If you can afford it, feel free to visit one of these stores every month or so to stock up on the items listed in each week's lesson. But by purchasing just a little bit each week, you'll still be able to come out ahead in the long run.

A couple more things before you get started. First, if you reach a lesson where you've already earned the merit badge, so to speak, that's fine, but don't just take the week off. Either move on to a new lesson or revisit a past one. Idle hands and all that. Second, consider yourself free to work ahead, too. If a particular lesson and assignment take you only a short time to accomplish, go ahead and move to the next one, if you'd like. It's far better to work ahead than to fall behind.

Finally, should you at any time need encouragement, have a question, or just want some guidance, you're welcome to e-mail me: Jim@Survival Weekly.com. I'm happy to do whatever I can to help you achieve your preparedness goals.

SECTION I
THE BASICS

WEEK 1

LISTS, LISTS, AND MORE LISTS

To move forward, it's best to know where you are now. After all, it's difficult to give someone directions if you don't know where he or she is starting out from, right?

Your first assigned task on your journey to preparedness is to make lists of what you already have in your home or what you otherwise have available to you. Some folks prefer to handwrite such lists in a spiral notebook. Others may choose to make some sort of spreadsheet on their computer. There are even apps for smart phones that will do this as well. I suggest going the pen-and-paper route. This way, you can still access the information during a power outage.

Below are the details about the lists I want you to make.

FOOD STORAGE

Go through every cupboard, each shelf, and even your fridge and freezer. Mark down every single edible item in your home, from individual spice containers all the way to that turkey you bought on sale before Thanksgiving. Next to each item on your list, write down how old it is, estimating as needed. Be diligent in your efforts; don't overlook anything. The idea here is, what if a disaster hit and what you have on hand is *all* the food you have for your family? No emergency runs to the grocery store; all crops you may have are pulled. Naturally, this list is in flux, since it'll change as you prepare meals and such. That's OK, don't worry about it. Just write down everything you have on hand at the time you're making the list. The goal is simply to get a good idea of where you're starting when it comes to food storage.

SAMPLE FOOD STORAGE LIST

- ❏ 4 cans beans
- ❏ 10 cans soup
- ❏ 2 pounds flour
- ❏ 1 pound sugar

WATER STORAGE

Next, list how much water you have stored. Include water bottles you may have scattered throughout the house and in the fridge. Find out the capacity of your water heater as well as your toilet tanks. If you have rain barrels and they're holding water, go ahead and add them as well. If you have water-purification equipment, such as a Berkey filter or purification tablets, list them here, too.

SAMPLE WATER STORAGE LIST

- ❏ 10 gallons bottled water
- ❏ 50 gallons water heater water
- ❏ 30 gallons rain-catch water
- ❏ 30 water-purification tablets

FIRST AID/MEDICAL SUPPLIES

Adhesive bandages, alcohol, hydrogen peroxide, gauze, over-the-counter medications, anything medical related should all go on this list. For things that have a use-by date, such as meds, include that in your list.

SAMPLE FIRST AID/MEDICAL SUPPLIES LIST

- ☐ 3 boxes (100-count each) adhesive bandages
- ☐ 4 tubes antibiotic ointment
- ☐ 5 packages rolled gauze
- ☐ 1 blood pressure cuff

HYGIENE

Here, I want you to include how many rolls of toilet paper you have, how much soap and shampoo, and how many other basic necessities. Sure, humans survived centuries without deodorant, but it sure is nice to have, isn't it? Especially if you have teenage boys in the house. Don't forget toothpaste, toothbrushes, and floss.

SAMPLE HYGIENE LIST

- ☐ 6 bars soap
- ☐ 2 bottles shampoo
- ☐ 2 packages baby wipes
- ☐ 34 rolls toilet paper

TOOLS

Include hand tools as well as battery-operated or electric power tools. Keep in mind that anything that runs on power might be of limited use to you in a "grid down" event. Yes, duct tape is a tool and should be included. Other types of tape? Um, not so much.

SAMPLE TOOL LIST

- ☐ 1 curved claw hammer
- ☐ 1 straight claw hammer
- ☐ 3 standard pliers
- ☐ 2 channel-lock pliers
- ☐ 6 slotted screwdrivers (various sizes)

MISCELLANEOUS

Here's where you list the odds and ends. Include anything that you feel will be an asset during or immediately after a disaster and that wasn't covered previously. Things like batteries, camping equipment, propane grills, that sort of stuff.

SAMPLE MISCELLANEOUS LIST

- ❑ 1 gas grill
- ❑ 2 propane tanks for grill (1 filled, 1 empty)
- ❑ 2 bags charcoal
- ❑ 1 tent

Please realize that making these lists isn't something you can accomplish in just an hour or so. Like anything else, to do the job right takes time and effort. Once these lists are complete, take a well-deserved break.

The next step is to determine the shelf lives of what you have on hand. With some foods, that's rather easy. But for many items, that can be difficult to figure out. And I'm not talking about the so-called best-by dates printed on the packages here, either. I'm referring to how long the items will actually last. Do some homework to determine how long foods and other items will last, then go back through your lists and determine as best as you can when the items you currently have will no longer be viable. Obviously, as you acquire more supplies, you'll want to use the oldest items first.

WEEK 1 ASSIGNMENTS

TASKS

☐ Create your master lists—food, water, first aid, hygiene, tools, miscellaneous. Keep them handy and add to or edit them as you go along in your daily life. No, you don't have to jot down a note every time you use a teaspoon of garlic powder. But as you use up supplies or add to them, adjust the lists accordingly.

SAVINGS

☐ Start your Prepper Savings Account by setting aside $20.

Total Prepper Savings Account: ☐

WATER STORAGE

☐ Begin storing water for emergencies. Either purchase a case of bottled water or fill two empty 2-liter soda bottles (2 liters is roughly a half gallon) per person. Put them in the back of a closet or in the basement, somewhere cool and dark, to inhibit the growth of bacteria, mold, and other nastiness on or inside the bottles.

Total Water Storage: ☐

GROCERY LIST

- ☐ 3 cans vegetables, your choice
- ☐ 2 cans fruit, your choice, but stick with those packed in water or juice, rather than syrup
- ☐ 2 cans meat (tuna, chicken, beef), your choice
- ☐ 2 cans soup, your choice, but not condensed (they require water)
- ☐ 1 canister oatmeal or 1 box flavored instant oatmeal
- ☐ 1 treat, such as a bag of chips or hard candy

☐ **WEEK COMPLETED**

Date:_____

WEEK 2
OUT WITH THE OLD

Most of us would agree that we have . . . way . . . too . . . much . . . stuff. Clothes, books, movies, gadgets, paper clutter, the list goes on and on. The typical American home is just swimming in stuff we don't need, don't use, and could easily get rid of without ever missing it.

This week, you're going to start purging. See, preps require not only investments of time and money but also space. Having a year's worth of food on hand is wonderful, but do you want all of it sitting in boxes in your living room?

This is one assignment you won't likely be able to accomplish in just one week. You'd quickly become overwhelmed trying to do that. Instead, make this an ongoing project and work on it a little at a time.

Start with your coat closet. My own rule of thumb when it comes to clothing and outerwear: If I haven't worn it in the last year, away it goes. Naturally, you may have some specialized gear, and you don't need to get rid of that. But you don't really need six different winter parkas, five light jackets, and four pairs of boots. That vacuum cleaner that stopped working three years ago? Either fix it this week or get rid of it. The bags for the vacuum cleaner you owned ten years ago and don't fit what you have now? Bye-bye.

From there, move through the rest of the closets in your home. If the clothes don't fit right now, toss them in a box. The only exception should be if you have kids and you plan to pass down clothes from one child to another. Otherwise, get rid of them. The clothes, not the kids.

Eventually, you need to go through every closet, every drawer, every shelf in your home. Think about it like this—if you get rid of something, you no longer need to dust it, store it, or deal with it.

Supplies for a hobby you gave up years ago? See ya later!

Movies you've seen and realistically don't plan to watch again? That's precious shelf space right there! This goes double for those of you who still have VHS movies but don't have a working VCR!

Books? OK, this is the one I struggle with the most. I have tons of books I haven't read yet. I have boxes of books I've read and hope to read again someday. I also have shelves and shelves of books that I should get rid of. And I'm doing so, but very slowly.

What do you do with all this stuff that you want to go away? Movies, books, and other things that are still in decent shape you might consider selling on eBay or Facebook Marketplace. If you go that route, take whatever money you make and put it toward preps.

For stuff that isn't quite as good, you might think about unloading it at a rummage sale in a couple of months. But promise yourself that anything that doesn't sell still has to go, one way or another. Whatever is left can go to Goodwill, the Salvation Army, or the trash (which is probably where much of it truly belongs).

WEEK 2 ASSIGNMENTS

TASKS

☐ Begin wherever you like in your home and start purging. Get rid of the stuff you don't need to make room for the stuff you do. Be vicious and cutthroat. Sell what you can and put the money toward prepping. If it won't sell, it goes to thrift stores, recycling, or the trash.

SAVINGS

☐ Add $10 to your Prepper Savings Account.

Total Prepper Savings Account: ☐

WATER STORAGE

☐ Store 1 gallon (or two 2-liter bottles) of water per person or a case of bottled water for the household.

Total Water Storage: ☐

GROCERY LIST

☐ 3 cans vegetables, your choice

☐ 2 cans fruit, your choice, but stick with those packed in water or juice, rather than syrup

☐ 1 can chili or stew, your choice

☐ 1 package or jar gravy, your choice

☐ 1 jar peanut butter (if allergies are an issue, substitute an allergen-free version, such as sunflower butter)

☐ 1 box granola bars, protein bars, or equivalent

☐ 1 gallon cooking oil (vegetable oil is preferred, for longer shelf life)

☐ **WEEK COMPLETED**

Date:_____

WEEK 3
BASIC WATER STORAGE

Clean, potable water is a life necessity. Our bodies need it to survive. We use it to clean ourselves, preventing illness and infection. We also use it to prepare food. Having plentiful water after a disaster cannot be over-emphasized.

Experts say that we'll need 1 gallon of water per person per day. To my way of thinking, that's almost absurdly minimal. I'd suggest at least 1½ to 2 gallons. More is always better.

The problem is that water is heavy and can be difficult to store in mass quantity. You can't shrink it down, either. It takes up a lot of space.

CALCULATE YOUR WATER NEEDS

Regardless of where you live, at a minimum, your family should have ten days' worth of potable or purifiable water per person on hand at any time. For a family of four, that amounts to 80 gallons of water. That's four 20-gallon water bottles. If you have limited storage space in your home, that might be the maximum you can store.

If you live in an area that's susceptible to catastrophes like hurricanes, blizzards, or earthquakes that could disrupt water supply for up to a month, you should plan to have even more water on hand.

Discuss with your family what you can realistically store in the space you have. If you follow all the storage goals in the weeks to come, you'll end up with about 52 gallons of water per person. That's potentially enough for three full months of off-the-grid (and pipes) living. If you don't have the space to store that much water, simply come up with a realistic, safe goal and then cut off your storage there. Don't forget to rotate your water supply if you're not purchasing sealed water. That'll keep your water safe and potable.

Look back to the list you made for how much water you have stored right now. Did you include the contents of your water heater? The average water heater holds about 30 gallons. That's enough to last a family of four a few days, and it's likely already there, without any planning on your part. Something to keep in mind, though, is that the last few gallons of that water are likely to be filled with sediment and such, unless your water heater is brand-new.

How many days could you last on the water you have stored right now? Do the math, I'll wait. If you have four people in your family and you have 40 gallons stored, at 2 gallons per day, you have enough for five days. And that's figuring nothing more than occasional sponge baths for cleanup.

What are the best ways to store water? I like to use cleaned-out soda and juice bottles. A 2-liter bottle is roughly a half gallon. I like them because they're both easy to store and not too cumbersome to use as is. There are, of course, containers specially made for storing water. I know several discount retailers that sell 7-gallon containers in their sporting goods sections, and those containers are nice to have. Most of them have a built-in spigot, which makes them easy to use. But again, water is heavy, and even a 7-gallon container takes a bit of oomph to move.

You could, of course, purchase commercially bottled water. But this can be expensive, and the water isn't much better than what's available in many homes free from the tap. That said, for some people, this might be the most feasible option.

Some folks advise that you should fill up your bathtub if you have the time to do so in an emergency. Not a bad plan, but how many of you have bathtubs clean enough to drink from at any given time? Of course, the water from the tub could be used for other purposes such as cleaning. What you'll want to do, though, is cover the filled bathtub to keep dust and other stuff out of the water. You can buy shower curtain liners at most dollar stores, and these would work well for that purpose. Just drape one over the tub and use books or something on the sides to keep it in place. If you do decide to fill your bathtub in an emergency, use only the cold faucet tap so you don't empty your water heater.

STORING YOUR WATER SAFELY

Your water should be stored in an easily accessible location. A basement is OK, *if* you're ready, willing, and able to carry that water up and down stairs. A better solution might be closets, pantries, that sort of thing. Someplace cool and dark is best.

Stored water also needs to be rotated regularly. Figure on a six-month schedule for rotation. Use the old water for houseplants, pets, and gardens. This doesn't apply to commercially bottled water. Kept sealed, this water will stay fresh pretty much forever.

THE WATERBOB

There's a product specifically designed for storing emergency water in the bathtub. The WaterBOB is a large plastic bladder that you roll out on the bottom of your tub, then fill from the faucet. It holds up to 100 gallons and comes with a handy siphon pump for transferring the water from the bladder to pitchers or jugs. Since it's sealed, there's no worry about debris falling into the water.

This would provide an excellent backup to your other water storage. But it should be considered only a backup. Obviously, it'll work only if the faucets are still running. Should you not be home at the time of the initial crisis, you might miss your window of opportunity to fill the WaterBOB. So keep storing water as instructed.

You can find the WaterBOB online at WaterBOB.com.

IMPORTANT NOTE ABOUT WATER STORAGE

As we go through each of the following sections, you'll be instructed to continue setting aside water for each member of the family, 1 gallon per person per week. However, it's also time to start rotating your supply to ensure that the water you're storing doesn't get stale.

Here's what you should do. Your water should be stored in such a way that you can easily determine which bottles are the oldest. Going forward, each week you'll remove 1 gallon from your storage and pour it into the water dish for the pets, use it for cleaning, or pour it into the garden. You'll then replace it with 2 gallons of fresh water. This replaces the gallon you took out as well as adds another gallon to storage. Note that this isn't a "per person" action. You're only adding 2 gallons of water in total. This way, you're constantly using up the oldest water as well as adding fresh to the stockpile. Note: Do *not* use milk jugs. They're not designed for long-term storage and degrade over time, soon developing pinholes in them. This very thing happened to my mother many years ago, leading to a huge mess in her basement.

But if you're storing purchased bottled water, rather than filling your own containers, there's no need to rotate the supply. Commercially bottled water will remain fresh as long as the seals on the bottles are not broken. So if you're storing cases of bottled water that you've bought at a warehouse store or grocery store, you can skip the whole rotation thing and just concentrate on building up your supply.

WEEK 3 ASSIGNMENTS

TASKS

❏ Determine a water storage goal, in terms of how long you feel you may need to provide for your own water needs in the event of a disaster. Calculate how much water you should have stored. Remember, you'll need 1½ to 2 gallons per person per day.

❏ Work out a plan to achieve your storage goal. Begin or continue to gather containers that will work for your situation. Be sure they're clean.

❏ Figure out a rotation schedule. What you want to avoid is dumping large quantities of your stored water all at once. The six-month rule is a guideline, not set in stone. Use up and replenish a few gallons each week to keep your supply fresh.

SAVINGS

❏ Add $10 to your Prepper Savings Account.

Total Prepper Savings Account: _____

WATER STORAGE

❏ Store 1 gallon (or two 2-liter bottles) of water per person or a case of bottled water for the household.

Total Water Storage: _____

GROCERY LIST

❏ 3 cans vegetables, your choice
❏ 2 cans fruit, your choice, but stick with those packed in water or juice, rather than syrup
❏ 2 cans meat (tuna, chicken, beef), your choice
❏ 2 cans soup, not condensed (they require water)
❏ 1 jar jelly or fruit preserves
❏ 1 jar pasta sauce, your choice
❏ 1 box or canister table salt
❏ 1 package nuts, dried fruit, or trail mix

❏ **WEEK COMPLETED**

Date:_____

WEEK 4

FINANCIAL PREPS

This is an area that far too many preppers overlook. Financial emergencies—including things like sudden job loss, unexpected vehicle repairs, and medical bills—are incredibly common. Financial preps should be a vital component of your overall preparedness plan.

The four pillars of financial preparedness are debt reduction, emergency savings, retirement planning, and the Death File. Let's briefly look at each one.

DEBT REDUCTION

Every dollar you spend on interest is a dollar you can't spend on something more practical or fun. Many of us are seemingly drowning in debt, and it can feel like we'll never get out from under it.

Do everything you can to pay your bills on time, every time. Even just one late-payment fee can really hurt you. Many creditors offer online payment arrangements, including scheduling payments in advance. Paying on time will also increase your credit score, which is always a good thing.

Consider calling a customer service rep at your credit-account companies and asking if there's anything they can do to help you get the balance paid down faster, such as a temporary interest rate reduction. The worst they can do is say no.

As for actually paying the debts off, one method that works well for many is called the debt snowball method. It's been around a long time. I remember my parents using that approach back in the early 1980s. Make a list of all your debts and rank them by amount owed. Each month, pay as much as you can afford toward the debt with the smallest balance, while also making the minimum payments on the other balances. Keep doing this until that one debt is paid in full. Then take what you were paying on that and put it toward the next one on the list. Lather, rinse, repeat. It takes time, especially if you have a lot of debt, but it works.

EMERGENCY SAVINGS

It's a whole lot easier to talk about than to do, but everyone really should have some sort of emergency fund set up. All too often, we get hung up on the idea of saving money because we don't have a way to save a lot of it all at once. But just like with food storage, a little at a time adds up.

Focus on the nickels and dimes. Combine errands with the car to conserve gas. Keep the thermostat a little lower in the winter and a little higher in the summer. Learn how to cook from scratch so you don't have to rely on takeout as often. Put these little budget savings into your emergency fund account.

Each day, put all your spare change into a jug. When you can hardly lift the container with one hand, take it to the bank to cash it in. Put half in your emergency savings and half toward something fun.

Maybe you could limit or outright quit habits that have a negative impact on your health, such as smoking. Been there, done that myself. I smoked for over twenty years before I finally gave it up. Given the price of tobacco, even just a few packs a week is a pretty serious chunk of a household budget.

Back in week 2, we talked about purging unwanted items from the home. If you're able to sell any of it, put at least some of that money into your emergency fund.

RETIREMENT PLANNING

While many preppers seem to want to rely on the world collapsing before they hit retirement age, it might be a better idea to hedge that bet. You can explore a few different strategies when it comes to saving for your retirement. These include employer retirement savings, such as 401(k) accounts, individual retirement accounts (IRAs), and pension plans where available.

Dabbling in investments can also reap some rewards, but they aren't without risk. If you know what you're doing and play your cards right, you can do very well. This is typically a long-term approach.

For a long time, real estate was seen as a solid investment. Being a landlord and managing one or more rental properties as a side gig can bring in extra income that can be put toward retirement savings. However, as someone who spent several years working as a process server and who had to serve eviction notices on a regular basis, I can tell you with some authority that investing in rental property is far from a sure thing. A good tenant can be worth their weight in gold, while a bad tenant can cost you thousands.

I strongly advise you to speak with a retirement advisor about your individual situation and come up with some strategies that will work for you.

THE DEATH FILE

We're going to get into this later in the book. Suffice it to say for now that the Death File is essentially information and instructions your family will use after you've passed. There's nothing morbid about it. Death is a part of life, and we should plan for it just like we plan for everything else.

WEEK 4 ASSIGNMENTS

TASKS

☐ Sit down and outline a debt reduction strategy. Use the debt snowball method if needed.

☐ Talk with your family about the need for an emergency savings fund and brainstorm ways to add to it.

☐ Make an appointment with a retirement advisor to speak with them about strategies you can explore that are well suited for your family.

SAVINGS

☐ Add $20 to your Prepper Savings Account.

Total Prepper Savings Account: [   ]

WATER STORAGE

☐ Store 1 gallon (or two 2-liter bottles) of water per person or a case of bottled water for the household.

Total Water Storage: [   ]

GROCERY LIST

☐ 3 cans vegetables, your choice

☐ 2 cans fruit, your choice, but stick with those packed in water or juice, rather than syrup

☐ 1 can chili or stew, your choice

☐ 1 package or jar gravy, your choice

☐ 1 box baking mix, preferably the type that doesn't require eggs, milk, or other ingredients

☐ 1 box (12 packages) ramen noodles

☐ 1 pound white rice

☐ **WEEK COMPLETED**

Date:_____

MONTH 1 TOTALS

You've made it through your first month of prepper planning! This is what you should have learned and what you should have stored.

TASKS

☐ Created master lists of various categories of supplies to give you a good idea of where you stand

☐ Begun clearing out unwanted or unneeded items in the home, to make room for necessary supplies

☐ Started your food and water storage plans

☐ Begun working on your financial preparedness

PREPPING SAVINGS

☐ You should have $60 set aside for future prepping purchases.

WATER

☐ You should have at least 4 gallons of water for each member of the family.

GROCERIES

☐ 12 cans vegetables
☐ 8 cans fruit
☐ 4 cans meat
☐ 4 cans soup
☐ 2 cans chili or stew
☐ 2 packages or jars gravy
☐ 1 box baking mix
☐ 1 box (12 packages) ramen noodles
☐ 1 pound white rice
☐ 1 jar jelly or fruit preserves
☐ 1 jar pasta sauce
☐ 1 canister table salt
☐ 1 package nuts, dried fruit, or trail mix
☐ 1 jar peanut butter
☐ 1 box granola bars, protein bars, or equivalent
☐ 1 gallon cooking oil
☐ 1 canister oatmeal or 1 box flavored instant oatmeal
☐ 1 treat, such as a bag of chips or hard candy

WEEK 5
BUG OUT BAGS

The ideal in most situations is what we refer to as sheltering in place. Unless you have a fully stocked retreat elsewhere, home is generally where all your preps are located. You should plan to remain at home unless and until such a time that you're unable to do so.

Many reasons can cause you to evacuate at a moment's notice. While residents are typically evacuated for only a short period of time, one never knows how those situations may play out. A few years back, a huge fire broke out at a factory a couple of counties away from where I live. Quite a bit of toxic smoke and debris were blanketing the area, and residents were forced to flee. Many of them weren't allowed to return for at least a day or two.

In situations like that, you have to get on the road and away from the area quickly.

Because you won't have time to go through the house and neatly pack your belongings, you should prepare an evacuation kit, what we often refer to as a "bug out bag."

The idea behind the bug out bag presupposes that you have someplace to go (family member's home, hotel, etc.) and stay for a few days. The kit isn't meant for roughing it but rather to give you the materials and tools you'll need to be away from home for a while.

The bug out bag should be kept in an easily accessible location within the home, such as a closet. Put together one kit for each family member, though you might not need separate packs for each person.

Here's what you should have in your bug out bags:

- At least two complete changes of clothes for each person, with extra socks and underwear as well. If you can swing it, include an extra pair of shoes for each person. If you're roused out of bed in the middle of the night, some or all of you may end up shoeless on your way out the door.
- Maps of the area, including planned routes of evacuation and a list of local emergency shelters.
- Money (cash, coins, credit cards).
- Copies of important papers, such as insurance policies, proof of vehicle and home ownership, pet vaccination records, and identification.
- Copies of treasured family photos. You could scan them and save them on a thumb drive. Include current photos of every family member and family pet. For pictures of pets, the ideal is pictures of you with your pet. That'll go a long way toward proving ownership if that becomes an issue.
- Snacks like nuts and dried fruit, granola bars, and crackers.
- At least one, preferably two, water bottles for each person. Don't forget a good-quality water filter or another means of treating water, just in case the disaster causes problems with the water supply.
- Small first aid kit and an extra supply of any prescription medications that may be necessary.
- Hygiene supplies, such as toothbrushes, toothpaste, deodorant, bar of soap, and a washcloth. Including a roll or three of toilet paper is a good idea, along with extra feminine hygiene supplies.
- Flashlights will be welcome if the evacuation is at night and you end up on foot. Headlamps are even better.

☐ A portable radio, either battery or crank powered, will help you keep informed of what's going on.

☐ Extra batteries for any devices in the kit that require them. Remember, the idea behind an evacuation kit is simply to provide for your basic needs while away from home for a few days. It isn't intended for long-term survival.

WEEK 5 ASSIGNMENTS

TASKS

☐ Assemble a bug out bag for each family member. Use common sense: You won't need to include a separate portable radio for each person. The overall kit for each person will likely end up being fairly small, and you can probably pack several kits into one or two larger bags. Keep the bag(s) in a hall closet and make sure each family member knows where they are so they can quickly grab them on the way out the door.

☐ Plan ahead for potential evacuation. Talk with family members about the possibility of staying with them for a few days, and vice versa. Determine where emergency shelters are commonly opened in your area, such as in churches and schools. While these shelters are typically the last resort for the prepper, it's an option to be explored. The point is, plan out where you could go and how you'd get there.

SAVINGS

☐ Add $20 to your Prepper Savings Account.

Total Prepper Savings Account: [   ]

WATER STORAGE

☐ Store 1 gallon (or two 2-liter bottles) of water per person or a case of bottled water for the household.

Total Water Storage: [   ]

GROCERY LIST

- ❏ 3 cans vegetables, your choice
- ❏ 1 package dry soup mix, your choice
- ❏ 2 cans meat (tuna, chicken, beef), your choice
- ❏ 1 bag cornmeal
- ❏ 2 cans soup, not condensed (they require water)
  1 jar instant coffee (even if you don't drink coffee, this is a great barter item)
- ❏ 2 cans fruit, your choice, but stick with those packed in water or juice, rather than syrup

❏ **WEEK COMPLETED**

Date: _____

WEEK 6
TALKING TO YOUR IMMEDIATE FAMILY ABOUT PREPPING

This week, I want you to concentrate your efforts on getting your family to buy into disaster readiness. This is an often-cited problem preppers face—a spouse or other family member who just doesn't get it.

Prepping is hard work, and it's even harder when you're fighting against someone who doesn't think it's necessary. Harder yet when family members openly ridicule you or otherwise negatively express their opinions on the subject.

So how can you convince a spouse to get on board? Many people often liken prepping to buying insurance. Let's face it, insurance policies are one of the only things we ever buy in life and hope we never need to use, right? In fact, we'll sometimes go to great lengths to not to have to file a claim. Ever been in a fender bender? If the damage is slight, you'd gladly pay for the damage out of your own pocket so your insurance company doesn't raise your rates.

Prepping is sort of like insurance. We set aside food and supplies against what might happen, but we hope and pray we never really need to use that stuff in an emergency. The difference between prepping and insurance, though, is we can still use our preps as we feel necessary, without incurring the wrath of an insurance agent. In fact, it's encouraged that you regularly use and rotate your supplies to keep them fresh.

Another argument you can make, particularly about food storage, is about the ability to eat tomorrow at today's prices. Have you been to the grocery store lately? Prices sure aren't coming down on anything, are they? It doesn't seem all that long ago that I could buy ground beef for about a dollar a pound on sale. Now, I'm lucky if I can find it for six times that price. If I buy a jar of peanut butter for a few dollars today and it sits on my shelf until I go to make peanut butter cookies for Christmas and I find out that same jar now costs $5 at the store, I just saved myself money, right?

If the reason behind your spouse's reticence is less about the possible expense and more about thinking nothing will ever happen that might require the need for preps, you could talk about all the things that have happened recently to folks who thought that same thing. How many people living in Bosnia in the mid-1990s thought their government would collapse? How many folks living in North Carolina in 2024 worried a major hurricane would hit their area? Who in Japan would have ever even considered the devastation of the tsunami in 2011? Or talk about smaller-scale emergencies like multiple-day power outages in the winter or ice storms that strand you for days at home. Or what about a flu virus brought home by the kids that rampages through the house, keeping everyone home for a week. That last one hit my family once, and let me tell you, it was a whole lot of no fun for all involved.

Remember, too, that all it would take is one emergency close to home and many of those who pooh-poohed prepping will change their tune. When that happens, please be gentle with the "I told you so."

WEEK 6 ASSIGNMENTS

TASKS
☐ Have a heart-to-heart talk with your spouse, significant other, or any other family member who is opposed to prepping. Use some of the suggestions above to get them to understand your point of view.

SAVINGS
☐ Add $20 to your Prepper Savings Account.

Total Prepper Savings Account: [   ]

WATER STORAGE
☐ Store 1 gallon (or two 2-liter bottles) of water per person or a case of bottled water for the household.

Total Water Storage: [   ]

GROCERY LIST
☐ 3 cans vegetables, your choice
☐ 2 cans fruit, your choice, but stick with those packed in water or juice, rather than syrup
☐ 1 can chili or stew, your choice
☐ 1 package or jar gravy, your choice
☐ 1 box tea bags, your choice (even if you don't drink tea, these are great barter items)
☐ 1 box granola bars, protein bars, or equivalent
☐ 1 pound dry beans, your choice

☐ **WEEK COMPLETED**

Date:_____

WEEK 7
PACE PLANNING

Primary, alternate, contingency, and emergency (PACE) planning is a great tool for many areas of preparedness. This method was originally developed for communications, but it has far-ranging applications. Here's how I think of this strategy:

Primary—This is the best option available to you to solve the problem or accomplish the goal. It's the one you turn to as a default.

Alternate—This is the first backup. It should be commonly available and easy to use, but maybe it's slightly less optimal than your primary choice.

Contingency—This is your second backup option. This one might not be quite as reliable or convenient, but it's largely workable.

Emergency—This is the option of last resort, the Hail Mary pass you try when nothing else is available.

Here's how this works. Let's say we're planning for emergency evacuation from home and the way we're going to get from point A to point B. For the sake of discussion, we're looking at a family of four with two children under ten years old. The family also has two medium-size dogs.

Primary is the family minivan. It's comfortable, large enough for everyone to fit just fine. It's reliable and kept in good condition with routine maintenance.

Alternate is dad's commuter car. It's a little on the small size, so it's going to be cramped with everyone plus the dogs. But it'll get the job done. It gets good mileage, too, which is a bonus.

Contingency is the next-door neighbor's truck. He owns two trucks, one for work and another for personal use. The families have lived next to each other for several years and know each other pretty well, certainly well enough to ask to borrow a truck. And if nobody is home, you know where the spare keys are kept. That's probably a conversation you should have with them ahead of time, though. That's only fair, right?

Emergency is everyone hopping on bicycles, with the dogs running alongside.

PACE is applicable to most areas of preparedness planning. For example, if we're looking at starting a fire, it might work like this:

- **Primary** = disposable lighter
- **Alternate** = strike-anywhere matches
- **Contingency** = ferrocerium rod and striker
- **Emergency** = friction fire, such as a bow drill

One of the most common catchphrases or mottos in the prepper world is "Two is one, one is none." It has roots in the military, though tracing it to one original source gets murky. The idea is that you should have multiple means of fulfilling basic needs. Where PACE really shines is helping you to fill gaps in your plans. You don't necessarily have to come up with four distinct options for each and every need, but you should absolutely have more than one backup.

WEEK 7 ASSIGNMENTS

TASKS

☐ Begin using the PACE methodology as you develop your preparedness plans. As you find gaps or holes, fill them as best you can.

SAVINGS

☐ Add $15 to your Prepper Savings Account.

Total Prepper Savings Account: [   ]

WATER STORAGE

☐ Store 1 gallon (or two 2-liter bottles) of water per person or a case of bottled water for the household.

Total Water Storage: [   ]

GROCERY LIST

☐ 3 cans vegetables, your choice

☐ 2 cans fruit, your choice, but stick with those packed in water or juice, rather than syrup

☐ 2 cans meat (tuna, chicken, beef), your choice

☐ 2 cans soup, not condensed (they require water)

☐ 1 box crackers, your choice

☐ 1 jar pasta sauce, your choice

☐ 1 pound pasta, your choice

☐ **WEEK COMPLETED**

Date:_____

WEEK 8
SPECIAL PREP CONSIDERATIONS: CHILDREN

For many of us, our families are the reason for our prepping. We want to do everything we can to make sure they're safe, no matter what happens in our lives. When it comes to our children, especially young kids, there are a few needs we should ensure we address.

NUTRITION

Often, as we're starting out with food storage, we stick to the bare essentials, and we may overlook the real nutritional needs of our children in particular. A good multivitamin can help bridge the nutritional gap when we're feeding our children strictly from our food storage.

Growing bodies also need a lot of protein and calories. While we might poke a bit of fun at how much teenagers eat, the reality is that their bodies need all that food to grow. Be sure you have ample food stored for your family.

Also, don't forget that kids are the pickiest eaters on the planet. Granted, when push comes to shove, they'll eat whatever you put in front of them if they're hungry enough. But going through the arguments about how they liked potatoes just fine two days ago and it makes no sense that they now can't stand them will accomplish nothing other than increasing stress in an already stressful situation. Provide variety in the foods you store and don't overlook a bit of junk food here and there.

HYGIENE

With young children in the family, this refers to diapers and wipes, as well as a way to either clean or dispose of them. Even those parents who are die-hard users of cloth diapers might consider investing in a box or two of disposables. In many disasters, it'll be far easier to dispose of them than it will be to use possibly precious water resources to clean reusable ones.

You know how you can tell a male child has truly hit puberty? The clouds of body spray that fill the bathroom and hallway. Face it, kids can just plain stink. Plan ahead for providing a way to wash up regularly.

If you have girls in the family who get their period or may begin doing so soon, plan for that as well and stock up on the necessary supplies.

ENTERTAINMENT

Every parent dreads rainy summer days, waiting for the inevitable complaint, "There's nothing to do!" Now, imagine those days of being cooped up going on and on for a week, two weeks, or even longer. Shudder. Invest in some cheap board games, toys, books, and other distractions and keep them boxed up until they're really needed. Do what you can to update that box from time to time to keep the contents age appropriate. The eye rolling from a fifteen-year-old being presented with Chutes and Ladders may prove deadly.

EDUCATION

If you're planning for extreme long-term scenarios, don't forget to include the education of your children. Invest in homeschooling texts and other resources in the basic subjects like math, science, and history. Stock up on extra notebooks, pens, pencils, and other supplies during back-to-school sales.

Above all, get your kids involved with prepping. Don't make it a mystery to them. At the appropriate ages and maturity levels, teach them skills like canning, tracking, shooting, first aid, and fire building. If you have active Scout troops in your area, they can be a great way to help your kids learn wilderness skills. Obviously, there will be some things that you want to hold off on sharing with your children until they are much older, such as perhaps the extent of your food storage. It takes a while before young people truly appreciate the importance of operations security (also referred to as OPSEC).

Let them help with packing their own bug out bags, planning and preparing meals, and building snow caves. Teach them actual skills in addition to basic sentence structure. Show them how to change the oil in the car, then have them do it next time while you supervise. Get them involved with home projects so they learn how to turn a screw and cut a board. Make them understand that the best meals don't go from a box into the microwave.

WEEK 8 ASSIGNMENTS

TASKS

☐ Make it a point this week to talk about prepping with your children, keeping the discussion age-appropriate. For young children, one outstanding resource is the Sesame Street website (SesameWorkshop.org). It has a ton of great information on how to discuss disasters with children. As you go forward in your prepping, be sure you're accounting for any special needs of your children, including diet, clothing, and medications.

SAVINGS

☐ Add $10 to your Prepper Savings Account.

Total Prepper Savings Account: ☐

WATER STORAGE

☐ Store 1 gallon (or two 2-liter bottles) of water per person or a case of bottled water for the household.

Total Water Storage: ☐

GROCERY LIST

- ☐ 3 cans vegetables, your choice
- ☐ 2 cans fruit, your choice, but stick with those packed in water or juice, rather than syrup
- ☐ 1 can chili or stew, your choice
- ☐ 1 package or jar gravy, your choice
- ☐ 1 box powdered milk
- ☐ 1 box (12 packages) ramen noodles

☐ **WEEK COMPLETED**

Date:_____

WEEK 9
SPECIAL PREP CONSIDERATIONS: PETS

Whether you view your animals as something akin to employees who are there to do a job, or (like me) you see them truly as members of your family, you need to plan ahead for their needs during and after a disaster. Our pets rely on us to provide them with food, water, and shelter, as well as to take care of any medical needs.

For our discussion here, I'm concentrating mostly on dogs and cats, though the same principles apply to whatever critters you may have. But given that dogs and cats are the most popular family pets, I focus on them.

Our pets have the same needs as we do, so let's take those one at a time.

WATER

Figure an average of 1 gallon of water per pet per day. Obviously, toy breeds will require less water than, say, a Siberian husky, so adjust the amount accordingly. The important thing is to have ample water stored for your pets as well as the rest of your family.

FOOD

You should easily be able to calculate how much food your pet will need per day. While you could theoretically feed your pet scraps from your own meals, that's probably not the wisest plan. First, you might not have scraps to spare. Second, a sudden change in diet may lead to some intestinal issues with your pet.

FIRST AID AND MEDICAL CARE

Basic first aid supplies for pets include gauze wraps, alcohol for disinfection, bandage tape, and antibiotic ointment. If your pet has specific medical needs, such as special medication, talk to your vet about acquiring a small supply to keep on hand for emergency use.

COLLAR AND ID TAGS

Make sure your pet has a collar with appropriate ID and vaccination tags on it. Keep an extra set, with a spare leash for dogs, in your pet emergency supply kit. Make copies of ownership paperwork, vaccination records, and medical records and keep this information with your kit.

RECENT PHOTO OF YOU AND YOUR PET

This is very important. Should you and your pet become separated, having a recent picture of the two of you together will help prove ownership. And a photo will help other folks locate your pet if it becomes lost.

PET CARRIER

Should you need to evacuate, transporting your pet in a crate or pet carrier might be beneficial. The crate should be big enough that your pet can stand, turn, and lie down comfortably. Don't forget a soft blanket as well as a toy or two.

SANITATION

For cats, make sure you have an ample supply of litter for their box. For dogs, if you run into a situation in which you won't be able to let them outside for some reason, a stack of old newspapers along with cleaning supplies may be necessary.

Keep in mind that many public emergency shelters will not allow you to bring in your pets, so plan ahead. Call around to area motels to see which ones are pet friendly. Also, talk to neighbors, friends, and family to discuss who might be able to help you with your pets should you need to evacuate without them.

WEEK 9 ASSIGNMENTS

TASKS

☐ Put together a pet emergency supply kit. Make sure to include all the items listed above, as well as any additional needs for your specific situation. When you start formulating your evacuation plans, be darn sure you've included your pets in the equation. Find out where you can go with your pets in an emergency. Be sure to keep them up-to-date on any vaccinations, too: Even if a shelter allows pets, it may not if the pet isn't current on all shots.

SAVINGS

☐ Add $10 to your Prepper Savings Account.

Total Prepper Savings Account: ⬚

WATER STORAGE

☐ Store 1 gallon (or two 2-liter bottles) of water per person or a case of bottled water for the household.

Total Water Storage: ⬚

GROCERY LIST

☐ 3 cans vegetables, your choice
☐ 2 cans fruit, your choice, but stick with those packed in water or juice, rather than syrup
☐ 2 cans meat (tuna, chicken, beef), your choice
☐ 2 cans soup, not condensed (they require water)
☐ 1 package dry soup mix, your choice
☐ 1 box instant potatoes
☐ 1 pound white rice

☐ **WEEK COMPLETED**

Date:_____

WEEK 10
BASIC FOOD STORAGE

Adequate food storage is one of the cornerstones of prepping. While the body can certainly last at least a few weeks without food, the latter part of that time frame will be decidedly less than pleasant. Food is what fuels the body, and in the aftermath of a disaster, you'll need all the fuel you can get.

Look back to the master food list you made during week 1. How many days could you realistically feed your entire family using only what you have on hand right now? Dr. Bruce Clayton, one of the true godfathers of modern survivalism, has said that if you don't have at least one full year of food stored, you're wasting your time. Obviously, if you're just starting out, amassing that much food seems more than a little daunting. Break it up into several easier-to-reach goals. Strive for enough food stored for a week, then two weeks, then a month, then three months. Keep setting the bar higher until you're satisfied with the amount of food you have stored.

When it comes to food storage, you want a mix of products. You need not, and should not, just go out and buy several pallets of freeze-dried products and call it a day. First of all, doing so will be extremely expensive. Further, proper rotation is a key element of any successful food storage plan. You need to use and restock your stored food regularly. Always use the oldest product first.

While dumping several boxes of freeze-dried food into your pantry isn't necessarily the worst idea in the world, you need to condition yourself and your family by introducing it into the diet gradually. Failing to do so could have a significantly negative impact on everyone's digestive systems. A better idea is to work on stocking up on the foods that your family already knows and enjoys, such as canned foods like veggies, pasta, stew, chili, and soup; dried goods like beans and rice; and staples like flour, sugar, salt, and spices.

Concentrate on buying things that are relatively cheap, to get the most bang for your buck. Look at not only the price but the number of servings as well. A can of condensed soup might cost less than a dollar, but you'll be lucky to get two servings out of it. Not a bad deal if you're feeding yourself, but if you have a spouse as well as growing kids, you'll need a bit more than just a can or two for a meal.

Rice is still relatively inexpensive. Dried beans are an excellent source of protein and easy to prepare. Beans, rice, and a can of peas, and you can feed your entire family for mere pennies per person.

We're not talking about gourmet meals here, obviously. Instead, focus on filling bellies with nutrition and calories.

How do you know how much you really need per day? An easy way to figure out your family's needs is to devise a meal plan for two full weeks. Don't worry about what you have in the house right now; this is all just hypothetical. Sit down with paper and pen and write out what your family might normally eat for breakfast, lunch, and dinner. Then add in one or two snacks as well, since I'm sure family members are used to having a quick bite between meals. Be as detailed as you can with these meals, estimating quantities of each ingredient that goes into the meal. Don't just write "tacos" for dinner on Tuesday. Figure out how much meat and other ingredients you normally use.

Creating a meal plan for two full weeks, then doubling each meal, gives you a fairly accurate estimate of what you'll need for a month to feed everyone. Granted, you may not have access to all the ingredients, such as fresh vegetables, but these figures give you a baseline, a starting point, for your food storage plans.

WEEK 10 ASSIGNMENTS

TASKS

☐ Examine your master list for food supplies and estimate how long you could feed your family on what you have on hand right now. Then determine your first food storage goal. Create menu plans to help guide your estimates. If you're at two weeks, shoot for a month. If you're already at a month, then go for two or three months. As we go forward with the lessons, use the items in the purchase category of the assignments as suggestions and substitute both the items and the quantities as needed to meet your food storage goals.

SAVINGS

☐ Add $15 to your Prepper Savings Account.

Total Prepper Savings Account:

WATER STORAGE

☐ Store 1 gallon (or two 2-liter bottles) of water per person or a case of bottled water for the household.

Total Water Storage:

GROCERY LIST

- ☐ 3 cans vegetables, your choice
- ☐ 2 cans fruit, your choice, but stick with those packed in water or juice, rather than syrup
- ☐ 1 can chili or stew, your choice
- ☐ 1 package or jar gravy, your choice
- ☐ 1 pound dry beans, your choice

☐ **WEEK COMPLETED**

Date:_____

SECTION II
SPRING

… WEEK 11

WATER FILTRATION AND PURIFICATION

Back in section I, we talked about the importance of storing water. Indeed, storing water is one of your ongoing assignments throughout this project. Running just slightly behind this in importance is having the ability to filter and purify additional water supplies. There are, of course, many natural sources of water, such as lakes, rivers, rain, and snow melt. But no matter how absolutely crystal clear that water may be, it should still be filtered and purified.

One of the best investments a prepper can make is to purchase a water-purification system. The filters you can buy at big-box retailers in the plumbing or housewares department aren't going to cut it. Those are more for improving taste than for removing waterborne pathogens. Head to the sporting goods department or go online. Sawyer and Grayl are two good-quality brands.

As you compare costs and brands, take a hard look at the specs for each unit. You're going to want something that will filter sufficient quantities of water to suit your needs. For example, if you have a family of five, you're probably going to want a system that will do more than a gallon an hour. You also want to consider the size of the organisms the system will filter out. You want a filter that will remove at least down to the 0.2–0.3 micrometer range. That will handle the bad critters like cryptosporidium and giardia. Look for filter products that have been tested and approved by the National Sanitation Foundation (NSF).

Unfortunately, such filtration systems don't work so well on viruses, which tend to be considerably smaller. With that in mind, you may want to incorporate an additional step of chemical treatment or boiling to ensure safe water.

There are also many ways you can purify water without using such devices.

BOILING WATER

Bring the water to a rolling boil. It used to be that experts recommended letting the water boil for several minutes, but now the latest information says that the water needs to be brought to a rolling boil for only a minute. Doing so is enough to kill off any harmful organisms. Naturally, this method requires enough fuel to boil large quantities of water as well as the time to not only boil the water but allow it to cool enough to handle or consume. When at all possible, though, use boiling to disinfect the water—it's the surest way to provide clean water. In fact, you might consider it a best practice to first filter the water through the product of your choice and then boil it as well, just to be safe.

BLEACH

Nonscented chlorine bleach will render questionable water potable. Add sixteen drops (1/8 teaspoon) of bleach to a gallon of water, swish it around, then let it sit for about a half hour. If the water still has a faint chlorine smell, you're good to go. If it doesn't, repeat the process. If the water is very cloudy or very cold, double the amount of bleach. Bleach is fairly inexpensive, but it does have a limited shelf life. Once the bottle is open, expect full potency for about six months before it begins to degrade.

You can make your own bleach mixture using calcium hypochlorite, also known as "pool shock." Here are the instructions for doing so, from the Environmental Protection Agency's website:

"The first step is to make a chlorine solution that you will use to disinfect your water. For your safety, do it in a ventilated area and wear eye protection. Add one heaping teaspoon (approximately ¼ ounce) of high-test granular calcium hypochlorite (HTH) to two gallons of water and stir until the particles have dissolved. The mixture will produce a chlorine solution of approximately 500 milligrams per liter. To disinfect water, add one part of the chlorine solution to each 100 parts of water you are treating. This is about the same as adding 1 pint (16 ounces) of the chlorine solution to 12.5 gallons of water. If the chlorine taste is too strong, pour the water from one clean container to another and let it stand for a few hours before use."[1]

This method is appealing because pool shock is very stable and lasts a long time if it's kept dry and cool. It can also be very inexpensive, especially during clearance sales at the end of summer. Given that you'll need to use only a very small amount to make your purification mixture, even one or two packages of pool shock will last you a good long time.

WATER-PURIFICATION TABLETS

Naturally, any camping supply store carries a wide range of water-purification tablets. These do work well, but you'll be able to disinfect only small amounts of water at a time. You'll go through quite a few tablets in just a few days if this is your primary disinfection method.

STRAW FILTERS

A few different filtration products are set up as straws. You just put the working end into the water and suck it up through the straw into your mouth. Most of these work well enough for limited use. But bear in mind that if you're going to need water for food prep, such as rehydrating freeze-dried foods, you'll be spitting mouthfuls of filtered water into

---

1. https://www.epa.gov/ground-water-and-drinking-water/emergency-disinfection-drinking-water.

your food. If that doesn't sound appealing, especially if you're going to be preparing food for the family, you might want to explore other options.

WATER BOTTLES

There are also different types of water bottles with the filtration unit built in, such as those sold by Grayl. Great to have and recommended, but don't count on using them to provide large quantities of clean water at any one time.

Of course, before disinfecting the water, it should be filtered to remove the larger stuff that may be present. One of the best ways to do this is to first let the water sit long enough for anything floating in the water to settle to the bottom of the container. Then pour the water through one or two coffee filters. I have also seen elaborate DIY setups using successive layers of small gravel, sand, and charcoal before going through coffee filters. If you have the time and the means, this is not a bad approach.

Clean water is absolutely essential to survival. While storing quantities of it is one of the first steps in a preparedness plan, you need to have the means to make found water potable as well. Few of us have the means to store all the water we'll need during and after a major disaster.

WEEK 11 ASSIGNMENTS

TASKS

☐ If you have the means to purchase a Grayl, Sawyer, or similar water-filtration unit, do so. If not, begin setting money aside for one.

☐ Begin gathering the supplies necessary for filtering and purifying water. These include coffee filters, pots for boiling, empty bottles, pool shock, bleach, and water-purification tablets. Always strive to have multiple methods available to you for any given task. As they say in the military, "Two is one, one is none."

SAVINGS

☐ Add $10 to your Prepper Savings Account.

Total Prepper Savings Account: [   ]

WATER STORAGE

☐ Store 1 gallon (or two 2-liter bottles) of water per person or a case of bottled water for the household.

Total Water Storage: [   ]

GROCERY LIST

☐ 3 cans vegetables, your choice
☐ 2 cans fruit, your choice, but stick with those packed in water or juice, rather than syrup
☐ 2 cans meat (tuna, chicken, beef), your choice
☐ 2 cans soup, not condensed (they require water)
☐ 1 canister oatmeal or 1 box flavored instant oatmeal
☐ 1 box granola bars, protein bars, or equivalent
☐ 1 sack (5 pounds) flour
☐ 1 pound white rice

☐ **WEEK COMPLETED**

Date:_____

WEEK 12

PLANNING YOUR GARDEN

Growing your own food not only is a vital component of self-sufficiency but saves you money on the grocery bill. There's also a distinct sense of satisfaction when you sit down to eat a meal with food that you produced yourself.

It doesn't matter what your living situation is: apartment, house, condo, whatever. There's always a way to grow something. Maybe the garden can't be quite as extensive as you'd like, but anything is better than nothing.

This is the time of year to begin planning your garden. If you've had gardens in the past, look at your successes and failures to determine what you need to work on this time around. On the other hand, if you're new to gardening, it's high time to get going on one.

If you don't have a large yard available to you, options include container gardening and square-foot gardening.

Container gardening is simply growing your plants in pots on your patio, porch, or driveway. Obviously, you're somewhat limited in what you can grow, since it'll all have to fit in pots. But since there's such a wide range of pot sizes, odds are you can find what you need to grow almost any common garden vegetable. Potatoes can be successfully grown in barrels, for example. You start with a layer of soil and compost. Plant your seed potatoes, and cover them with another layer of soil. As the plants sprout, keep all but the green plant covered, adding more and more soil as you go. At the end of the season, just tip over the barrel and harvest your taters.

Square-foot gardening is a little more complicated, but it's still doable for even the newest gardener. Many books and websites discuss this method in great detail. It involves building raised garden beds, filling them with prepared soil, and growing your crops in a grid pattern. This is an excellent approach if you have poor soil in your yard or if you have limited space. Square-foot gardening allows you to grow more vegetables in a smaller area.

However you approach the problem of space, begin by sketching out your proposed garden, with dimensions of length and width noted. Doing so will give you a good idea of what you have to work with as you plan your crops.

Next, determine what you want to grow this year. Again, if you've been through this particular rodeo before, you'll have a reasonable idea of what works in your area and what doesn't. If this is your first time around, consider getting in touch with your county extension office. The Master Gardeners there have one mission in life: to help folks like you.

Make a list of the vegetables you and your family enjoy. See what varieties you can grow locally. Don't forget fruits like strawberries. Consider trying new things, too. For example, I managed to live forty years without ever trying eggplant. There was no real reason for that; I just never got around to it. We decided to try growing eggplant and ended up with a fairly decent crop.

Unless you have unlimited space, you probably won't be able to grow as many different plants as you want. You'll have to prioritize. Consider concentrating on those vegetables that either historically grow tremendously well in your area or are appealing to your family.

Once you know what you want to grow, you'll need seeds. Whenever possible, get heirloom seeds. Heirloom seeds produce veggies and fruit that are "true," meaning the seeds from them can be planted next year to grow the same thing. Many, many seeds commonly sold in places like

Walmart are actually crossbreeds, and the seeds from your harvested crop will be sterile.

Numerous stores, online and otherwise, sell seeds. If you ask ten gardeners which places they like best, you'll probably get ten different answers. Your best bet is to ask people in your area who have gardens every year. You may luck out, and they'll give you a few seeds to get started. It never hurts to ask, as long as you're polite about it.

Another source is to look for local seed libraries. These are often set up inside public libraries in early spring. The way it works is that you select packets of seeds to plant. At the end of the season, you bring in seeds you've saved from what you harvested. This is typically free, though some locations may charge a nominal fee. Ask your local public library if they participate in the seed library program.

You also need to research the plants you wish to grow. Pay particular attention to plant size, best time to plant, and growing season. You need that information to best plan your garden. Look back at your garden sketch and start marking down where each type of plant will go. Balance out the plant sizes so you don't end up with big, bushy plants crowding out smaller ones. If you have a plant you can start in April and its growing season is seventy days, odds are you can use that space for a fall crop, too.

Make no mistake about it, gardening is rather labor-intensive. The planning, though, is where you can have all the fun without getting your hands dirty.

WEEK 12 ASSIGNMENTS

TASKS

☐ Research and plan your garden for this year. Begin acquiring seeds and organizing them. Store them in the order you'll be using them.

☐ Think about how you might be able to start the seeds indoors. Doing so can help increase your growing season as well as result in healthier plants. Really, you don't need much more than a table, plant trays, and a light.

SAVINGS

☐ Add $20 to your Prepper Savings Account.

Total Prepper Savings Account: ☐

WATER STORAGE

☐ Store 1 gallon (or two 2-liter bottles) of water per person or a case of bottled water for the household.

Total Water Storage: ☐

GROCERY LIST

☐ 3 cans vegetables, your choice
☐ 2 cans fruit, your choice, but stick with those packed in water or juice, rather than syrup
☐ 1 can chili or stew, your choice
☐ 1 package or jar gravy, your choice
☐ 1 jar peanut butter (if allergies are an issue, substitute an allergen-free version, such as sunflower butter)
☐ 1 jar pasta sauce, your choice
☐ 1 sack (4 pounds) sugar
☐ 1 pound pasta, your choice

☐ **WEEK COMPLETED**

Date:_____

WEEK 13
BASIC FIRST AID SUPPLIES AND TRAINING

Depending on the nature and extent of the disaster, immediate medical care may be nothing more than a fond memory. Most homes probably have a half-empty box of adhesive bandages (at best), as well as maybe a mostly empty tube of antibiotic ointment that expired around the time Clinton was dodging scandals. Homes with young children may have a bit more on hand, but likely nowhere near what's truly prudent.

Jane-Alexandra Krehbiel is a registered nurse and has years of practical experience in the field. Here is her recommended supply list for a well-stocked first aid kit for preppers, taken from her article "Basic Survival First Aid Kit," which first appeared on SurvivalWeekly.com.

BASIC SUPPLIES: WOUND

- ☐ Sterile 4×4 gauze, 1 large package for each family member
- ☐ Sterile 2×2 gauze, 1 large package for each family member
- ☐ Clean 4×4 gauze, 1 large package for each family member
- ☐ Clean 2×2 gauze, 1 large package for each family member
- ☐ Triangular bandage for each family member

- ❏ Large safety pins
- ❏ Roller gauze (6–8 rolls in a variety of sizes, used to secure dressings)
- ❏ Several chemical ice packs
- ❏ A variety of adhesive bandages
- ❏ Butterfly bandages
- ❏ Elastic bandages (both small and large)
- ❏ Spray bottle of normal saline (marketed as nasal saline) as gentle eye rinse
- ❏ 3 types of wound tape—paper, surgical, plaster (multiple uses)
- ❏ Sterile cotton swabs (about 200)
- ❏ Several packages of various protective medical masks

Note: Sterile gauze should be placed in contact with a wound, and the clean gauze can be used as padding over it. Remember that although this may sound like a lot of gauze, one serious wound can consume your supplies in just a few days.

BASIC SUPPLIES: GENERAL

- ❏ Neosporin cream, several tubes
- ❏ Hydrogen peroxide, 2 bottles
- ❏ Isopropyl alcohol, 2 bottles
- ❏ Povidone iodine, 2 bottles
- ❏ Diphenhydramine (Benadryl or generic) topical liquid for insect bites
- ❏ Needle-nose or fine splinter forceps (tweezers)
- ❏ Hemostats
- ❏ Dollar-store reading glasses as magnifiers if you're over 40, for removing splinters
- ❏ Glass thermometers in protective casing, both rectal and oral varieties
- ❏ Paramedic shears or blunt scissors

- ☐ Vinyl medical gloves (1–2 boxes); avoid latex because of possible allergies
- ☐ Plain, inexpensive, and deodorant-free sanitary napkins (multiple uses)
- ☐ Wire splint
- ☐ Rubber tourniquet

GENERAL MEDICATIONS

For each item I mention here, you should have a source of this medication for each family member. What I mean by this is that if you have infants and children, then you must stock Tylenol (acetaminophen) for each age group: drops for infants, chewables for children, and tablets for adults. The one exception is aspirin, which should not be given to children under eighteen without a physician's order, because in the presence of a viral syndrome, it's implicated in causing Reye's syndrome.

- ☐ Acetaminophen (Tylenol)
- ☐ Aspirin
- ☐ Imodium A-D
- ☐ Pepto-Bismol
- ☐ Diphenhydramine (Benadryl)
- ☐ Iosat for all family members, to be used in the event of a nuclear disaster
- ☐ Omeprazole
- ☐ Claritin dissolving tabs (loratadine)
- ☐ Ibuprofen (Advil, etc.)
- ☐ Ipecac bottle (to induce vomiting following certain poisonings)

Note: Always keep thirty days' worth of prescription medications you use on an ongoing basis.

SPECIAL NEEDS CONSIDERATIONS

DIABETES

- ❏ Prescription glucagon injection
- ❏ Ketodiastix
- ❏ Insulin syringes and your injectable insulin(s)
- ❏ Source of sugar or juice to treat hypoglycemia
- ❏ A spare glucometer with extra battery, strips, lancets, and supplies
- ❏ Insulin pump supplies, and pump batteries and peripherals (if you use a pump)

ALLERGIC EMERGENCIES (ANAPHYLAXIS)

Speak with your physician about the possibility that you or a family member should carry an Epipen.

ASTHMA

- ❏ Prescription inhaler
- ❏ Nebulizer (battery operated, in case of power failure)
- ❏ Medications and normal saline for nebulizer treatments

A well-stocked first aid kit will allow your family to treat many common injuries and illnesses. While there's no substitute for proper medical care administered by an experienced professional, there are certainly times when that just isn't feasible. When that happens, you'll have to make do with what you have.

It's important to recognize that all the supplies in the world won't do you much good if you don't know what to do with them. Everyone should take a basic first aid class, as well as obtain CPR training. On top of that, a Stop the Bleed class is also highly recommended. Many hospitals offer these classes. You can also reach out to your local fire department, as it will sometimes offer this training. If all that fails, contact your county emergency management department. Someone there should be able to guide you to a class or instructor.

WEEK 13 ASSIGNMENTS

TASKS

☐ Beginning this week, start assembling your first aid supplies. Use the list you made back in week 1 as a guide to what you have and what you need. Buy what you need as you can, and watch the sale fliers from your local stores. Stock up when the price is low.

☐ This week, I want you to look into first aid classes in your area. If feasible, sign up for one as soon as possible. Even if it is just a Stop the Bleed course, that will provide you with great training. But look for CPR classes as well as general first aid, too.

SAVINGS

☐ Add $10 to your Prepper Savings Account.

Total Prepper Savings Account: ☐

WATER STORAGE

☐ Store 1 gallon (or two 2-liter bottles) of water per person or a case of bottled water for the household.

Total Water Storage: ☐

GROCERY LIST

- ☐ 3 cans vegetables, your choice
- ☐ 2 cans fruit, your choice, but stick with those packed in water or juice, rather than syrup
- ☐ 2 cans meat (tuna, chicken, beef), your choice
- ☐ 2 cans soup, not condensed (they require water)
- ☐ 1 jar jelly or fruit preserves
- ☐ 1 box (12 packages) ramen noodles
- ☐ 1 bottle multivitamins
- ☐ 1 pound dry beans, your choice

☐ **WEEK COMPLETED**

Date:_____

WEEK 14

COMMUNICATIONS: TWO-WAY RADIOS AND CELL PHONES

In the aftermath of a disaster, it may become vitally important to communicate with family and loved ones. Obviously, you'll want to check on them to make sure they're OK, both right away and throughout the crisis. They'll want to do the same with you. So it's a good idea to take the time now to explore some of your options.

The ubiquitous cell phone may still work, at least in most situations. Most disasters are local in nature, affecting a relatively small area. But cell phone transmission lines can quickly become overcrowded, which makes it difficult to place calls. In that event, try sending text messages. Quite often, those transmissions will go through, since they use a different system. They're not ideal for communicating large amounts of information, but they'll do in a pinch.

Of course, that cell phone requires power to operate. Get into the habit of charging your cell phone daily. I plug in my phone every night at bedtime, letting it charge overnight. This way, if something were to happen, I'm at least starting the day with a full charge. But even that proactive measure might not be enough, and you could end up staring at a low-battery message on your phone. Fortunately, there are countless power packs on the market today. That said, I keep a wall adapter and power cord in my day pack so I can charge my phone if I'm somewhere that has power and an available outlet.

Another option for person-to-person communication is two-way radios. While similar in size and appearance to the walkie-talkies many of us played with in our youth, the FRS (Family Radio Service) and GMRS (General Mobile Radio Service) units are considerably more powerful. Like any other electrical gadget, they require power, but investing in a small solar-powered battery charger can help with that.

As a practical matter, there isn't much difference between FRS and GMRS radios. The biggest difference is that the GMRS ones require a license to operate. There are hybrid radios as well that will transmit and receive on both sets of frequencies. If you're unlicensed, just stick to the FRS frequencies.

What you can do is purchase a few pairs of these radios, giving one radio to each neighbor or family member in the immediate area and having all agree to use one specific channel to communicate with one another. These radios are not all that expensive and often go on sale at the beginning of summer for camping season as well as in the fall for hunting season.

As you shop around, don't worry about the ranges claimed on the packages. It might say the effective range is several miles, but that's true only if there's nothing larger than a blade of grass between you and the receiver. All these radios operate on "line of sight" and are, as a result, affected by trees, buildings, hills, and other obstructions. I would highly recommend experimenting in your area to determine exactly how far the radio signals will reach, and plan accordingly.

Something else to consider about these two-way radios is that they are by no means private. Anyone within range can turn on his or her own radio, tune to your channel, and hear everything being said. So I wouldn't rely on these units for any sort of private communication. Checking on Aunt Sally is one thing, but telling your right flank unit to sneak up on the enemy is quite another.

WEEK 14 ASSIGNMENTS

TASKS

☐ Begin shopping around for two-way radios. The goal is to have at least one radio for each family member, as well as one for each neighboring family. Play around with them to determine the actual range in your location.

☐ If you don't already have a cell phone, consider investing in a "pay as you go" model. You don't get locked into an unneeded or unwanted multiyear contract, but you still have the ability to use the phone during an emergency.

SAVINGS

☐ Add $10 to your Prepper Savings Account.

Total Prepper Savings Account: ☐

WATER STORAGE

☐ Store 1 gallon (or two 2-liter bottles) of water per person or a case of bottled water for the household.

Total Water Storage: ☐

GROCERY LIST

☐ 3 cans vegetables, your choice
☐ 2 cans fruit, your choice, but stick with those packed in water or juice, rather than syrup
☐ 1 can chili or stew, your choice
☐ 1 package or jar of gravy, your choice
☐ 1 box baking mix, preferably the type that doesn't require eggs, milk, or other ingredients
☐ 1 package dry soup mix, your choice
☐ 1 pound white rice

☐ **WEEK COMPLETED**

Date:_____

WEEK 15
HUMAN WASTE DISPOSAL

Where are you going to go when you have to, well, go? It isn't always as simple as finding a tree at the back of your yard. Proper disposal of human waste is essential in preventing illness. While toilets may still work even if the water pressure doesn't (you can fill the tank by hand), if the disaster goes on long enough, pump stations will get backed up and septic tanks will get full, which will cause overflows in homes. No, that won't be nearly as much fun as it sounds.

One option is to line the toilet with a garbage bag, replacing the bag as it gets full. The same principle applies when using a 5-gallon bucket. In fact, many camping supply stores now sell specially made toilet seats that will fit on those buckets. If the bucket is the option you're choosing, you could even dispense with the garbage bag liner and just use kitty litter or sand in the bucket to soak up the liquids.

In either case, you can help make the smell manageable by sprinkling the waste with powdered detergent or baking soda.

Of course, there are many different kinds of chemical toilets available, and you're welcome to purchase one or two of them. But the options mentioned above are considerably cheaper, which would free up funds to purchase other supplies.

Keep in mind that any container filled with human waste is going to be heavier than you might anticipate. Don't let the containers get so full you can't easily move them.

When it comes to disposing of the waste, there are basically two options: burning or burying. Each has its advantages and drawbacks.

If you bury the waste, it is out of sight (and smell). But that involves a considerable amount of work digging the holes and filling them in again. You'll need to do this as far as possible from any water source to prevent contamination. Figure at least a couple of hundred feet, more if feasible.

Burning the waste will involve less personal energy expenditure, since you won't be digging any holes. But you'll end up using lighter fluid or another flammable liquid to get the fire going, which is fuel you could use for other purposes.

Now, with all that said, there's also the possibility of building an old-fashioned outhouse or latrine pit. While this is not the worst idea in the world, heading out into minus-twenty-degree windchills to squat over a pit is no one's idea of a good time. If you decide to go this route, you'll want to situate the latrine at least two hundred feet from any water source. Dig a trench about six feet long, two feet wide, and a couple of feet deep. Keep the removed soil piled up nearby. To use, squat over the trench and do your business, then shovel some of the loose soil over the waste. If the crisis runs long enough that you end up filling the entire trench to about a foot from the top, dig another one.

While there are many alternatives to toilet paper, most of them are considerably less than ideal. Be sure to stock up on this vital supply, because you can never really have too much on hand. If you do run out of this essential and valuable resource, one of the best available options will be to cut old cotton shirts into squares. Flannel is ideal. Keep a covered bin in the bathroom for the used wipes. Plan to wash them at least every few days and do so with hot water and plenty of soap.

Be sure to also have a way to wash after using the facilities. One of my friends in the military has described how "ass and hand disease" laid out most of his buddies at some point during their tour of duty in the Middle East. It's a very real concern, as the lack of being able to wash hands is one of the main causes for disease in third world countries. Hit your local dollar store and stock up on hand sanitizer.

WEEK 15 ASSIGNMENTS

TASKS

- [ ] Determine how your family will be able to handle this admittedly somewhat uncomfortable situation. Look at your individual situation and decide how you'll solve the problem.
- [ ] Begin acquiring the necessary supplies, such as a 5-gallon pail and kitty litter. Set these supplies aside somewhere to ensure they don't get used for another purpose.

SAVINGS

- [ ] Add $15 to your Prepper Savings Account.

Total Prepper Savings Account: ☐

WATER STORAGE

- [ ] Store 1 gallon (or two 2-liter bottles) of water per person or a case of bottled water for the household.

Total Water Storage: ☐

GROCERY LIST

- [ ] 3 cans vegetables, your choice
- [ ] 2 cans fruit, your choice, but stick with those packed in water or juice, rather than syrup
- [ ] 2 cans meat (tuna, chicken, beef), your choice
- [ ] 2 cans soup, not condensed (they require water)
- [ ] 1 jar instant coffee (even if you don't drink coffee, this is an excellent barter item)
- [ ] 1 box granola bars, protein bars, or equivalent
- [ ] 1 pound pasta, your choice

☐ **WEEK COMPLETED**

Date:_____

WEEK 16
KEEPING CLEAN

The importance of keeping reasonably clean cannot be overemphasized. Being able to wash up not only is a huge boost to morale but also goes a long way toward preventing infections and illnesses.

Imagine being stuck at home for several weeks during a quarantine (self-imposed or otherwise). Faucets aren't working, so no running water is available. It's the height of summer, and no electricity means no air-conditioning. Each day you and your family are working hard in the garden to bring in needed food as well as making any necessary repairs or improvements to the home itself.

You are all constantly sweaty, dirty, and disheveled. And there's also an infant in the family going through perhaps a dozen diapers a day. A stink like that will get into your very soul. You need to plan ahead so you and your family members can clean up, at least somewhat.

Start with laying in a good supply of baby wipes, whether you have a young child in the home or not. These work great for quick sponge baths. They can also serve as toilet paper, of course, should you run out.

Next, stock up on soap and shampoo. While I fully realize bar soap can be used to clean hair as well as the body, generic shampoo isn't all that costly.

Toothbrushes, toothpaste, and mouthwash are all essential. Make sure you have plenty of extras on hand. Figure out how long a tube of toothpaste lasts your family and multiply that out so you have at least enough for a few months. Toothbrushes are supposed to last about six months, but they're cheap, so figure about five extras per family member. By the way, don't throw away the old ones. They're great for small cleaning projects.

Stick to unscented deodorants and avoid using body sprays in emergency situations. Trust me, I raised three teenagers. Body sprays are highly overrated when it comes to masking smells.

Hand sanitizer is critical. It'll allow you to wash your hands quickly after using the bathroom without expending water. But sanitizer does tend to dry out skin, so you might consider adding hand lotion to your shopping list.

A camp shower will probably be welcome after a few days without bathing. You can buy these at any decent sporting goods store or make your own. A 5-gallon bucket, painted black, will heat water nicely on a sunny day. If you're the handy sort, drill a hole in the bottom of the bucket and rig up a small hose-type fitting. Suspend the bucket above head level. Then attach a hose and nozzle to turn the water on and off. Or you could just have someone on a ladder dump water over you while you wash up.

Remember, you want to use rainwater for bathing purposes and not water you've stored for consumption.

WEEK 16 ASSIGNMENTS

TASKS

☐ Begin stocking up on things like soap, hand sanitizer, and other hygiene products. As I always say, watch the sale ads and use coupons if that gets you a better deal than buying generics. Your first goal is to set aside enough for three months. Once you've accomplished that, go for six months.

☐ Begin acquiring what you'd need for a camp shower, either by purchasing a kit or building your own.

SAVINGS

☐ Add $10 to your Prepper Savings Account.

Total Prepper Savings Account: ⬜

WATER STORAGE

☐ Store 1 gallon (or two 2-liter bottles) of water per person or a case of bottled water for the household.

Total Water Storage: ⬜

GROCERY LIST

☐ 3 cans vegetables, your choice

☐ 2 cans fruit, your choice, but stick with those packed in water or juice, rather than syrup

☐ 1 can chili or stew, your choice

☐ 1 package or jar gravy, your choice

☐ 1 box tea bags, your choice (even if you don't drink tea, this is a great barter item)

☐ 1 jar pasta sauce, your choice

☐ 1 pound dry beans, your choice

☐ **WEEK COMPLETED**

Date:_____

WEEK 17
OVER-THE-COUNTER AND PRESCRIPTION MEDICATIONS

I'm not going to enter into a debate about whether we've become a nation addicted to medications and why that may be the case or not. The fact of the matter is, many preppers and members of their families require daily doses of medications to survive. Add in the common over-the-counter medications that many people rely on when they become ill, and you're talking about a fair amount of pills and potions.

The problem with storing medications is that many don't have a very long shelf life, at least compared with other items we stockpile for later use. On average, a year is probably the longest you can expect a medication to be at full efficacy. But all meds are different, so do some research on the specific ones that you and your family take.

Complicating matters is the difficulty in setting aside mass quantities of prescription medications. Script meds are often expensive, even with insurance co-pays. There's a school of thought that suggests you may be able to save up a supply of meds by skipping a dose here and there. I cannot recommend this course of action at all. It's vital in many cases that you follow your physician's directions exactly.

A perhaps more feasible option is to pay close attention to when your prescription can be refilled and try to overlap that date with when you'll take your last dose of the current supply. For example, let's say next Wednesday is the soonest you can get a refill, but your current supply won't run out until next Friday. This would give you an extra two days of medication on hand. Do this a few more times, and you'll build up at least a small supply. Always take the oldest medications first, rotating your supplies to keep everything fresh.

If you're friendly with your physician, you could talk with him or her about your concerns. Explain that with all the talk in the media about getting disaster kits together, you're worried something could happen that would cut you off from a supply of your prescriptions. As long as you're not talking about narcotics or other controlled substances, your physician may be willing to work with you.

As for over-the-counter medications, think back on the last few years. What illnesses seemed to crop up most often? Stomach upset? Nasty head colds? What medications worked the best? Those are the things to stock up on. Again, though, don't go overboard and spend money on a large supply that may go bad before you truly need it.

Don't overlook antacids and general pain relievers and fever reducers like aspirin and ibuprofen. If anyone in your family has allergies, be sure to have the appropriate meds on hand.

Have young children? Make sure you have age-appropriate meds available.

Just about all medicines store best in a cool, dark location. I wouldn't necessarily toss everything into a corner of the basement, though. In most homes, a closet will serve just fine. Just be sure to rotate your supplies to keep things reasonably fresh.

Now, with all that said, I'd encourage everyone to look into natural remedies for common ailments as well as herbals and other options to replace some or all your prescription medications. I'm not saying to quit taking your meds cold turkey. Instead, partner with a physician who's agreeable to the use of such remedies. Beware that there could be some serious side effects if you start taking a natural remedy while still taking your prescription, even if the dose is reduced.

WEEK 17 ASSIGNMENTS

TASKS

☐ Make a list of all medications your family could possibly need during an extended crisis. Begin acquiring supplies of those meds as you find them on sale.

☐ Make a point of speaking with your physician about the need for additional quantities of prescription medications.

SAVINGS

☐ Add $20 to your Prepper Savings Account.

Total Prepper Savings Account:

WATER STORAGE

☐ Store 1 gallon (or two 2-liter bottles) of water per person or a case of bottled water for the household.

Total Water Storage:

GROCERY LIST

☐ 3 cans vegetables, your choice

☐ 2 cans fruit, your choice, but stick with those packed in water or juice, rather than syrup

☐ 2 cans meat (tuna, chicken, beef), your choice

☐ 2 cans soup, not condensed (they require water)

☐ 1 box crackers, your choice

☐ 1 box (12 packages) ramen noodles

☐ 1 pound white rice

☐ **WEEK COMPLETED**

Date:_____

WEEK 18

STAYING ON TOP OF MEDICAL AND DENTAL ISSUES

One of the first things that we'll likely miss after a total collapse is the relative ease with which we can obtain medical and dental care. Granted, dealing with our current health care system and insurance companies is no picnic, but it still beats the heck out of standing in line for hours on end to see the only medical professional (who might be a registered nurse, nursing assistant, or veterinarian) available for miles around.

As with anything else, an ounce of prevention is worth a pound of cure. While few people really enjoy visiting the doctor or the dentist, it's far better to get a handle on problems or potential issues early on instead of letting them fester and get worse and worse.

I freely admit that I absolutely abhor visiting the doctor and dislike going to the dentist even more. It's always a hassle to take time off work and hand over money out of my pocket. But none of us is getting any younger. As we age, it gets more and more important to stay on top of developing health problems.

Your focus this week is to see your doctor and dentist. You probably won't get an appointment for this coming week, but do what you can to get in soon. Get a complete physical done, including any recommended blood work. Get a dental exam, X-rays, and a cleaning if you can swing it.

If you have financial problems that are affecting your ability to get health or dental care, start setting money aside for that purpose.

With luck, you'll get a clean bill of health. If you don't, though, immediately start looking into natural remedies for any ailments or issues. Herbal remedies, folk medicine, that sort of thing. Remember, there may come a time when prescription medicines won't be available. Better to do the research now with all the resources available to you, such as the internet and public libraries.

It never hurts to speak to your doctor about alternative medical treatments as well. More and more physicians are recognizing the value of these approaches. If your doctor is dead set against anything other than popping pills, it might be time to look for a new medical provider.

WEEK 18 ASSIGNMENTS

TASKS

☐ Get in to see your doctor and dentist as soon as possible. Make a list of any issues you're concerned about and be sure to take the time to discuss them with your medical provider.

☐ If your physical condition is less than ideal, consider beginning some sort of exercise routine. There's no need to spend hours every day on this. Just some simple stretching exercises in the morning will take only about ten minutes and do you a world of good in a short period of time. If you're able to do so, fifteen to twenty minutes of walking every day will also be beneficial.

SAVINGS

☐ Add $15 to your Prepper Savings Account.

Total Prepper Savings Account: [   ]

WATER STORAGE

☐ Store 1 gallon (or two 2-liter bottles) of water per person or a case of bottled water for the household.

Total Water Storage: [   ]

GROCERY LIST

☐ 3 cans vegetables, your choice

☐ 2 cans fruit, your choice, but stick with those packed in water or juice, rather than syrup

☐ 1 can chili or stew, your choice

☐ 1 package or jar gravy, your choice

☐ 1 box powdered milk

☐ 1 pound dry beans, your choice

☐ **WEEK COMPLETED**

Date:_____

WEEK 19
NETWORKING

One key element to my own prepper/survivalist philosophy is that it's nearly impossible to survive a long-term societal collapse without assistance from others. I believe it's imperative to foster relationships now with family and neighbors to provide for better security and overall living conditions later.

There are reasons why it's helpful to have like-minded people around you now:

Pooling of resources: Perhaps you and two of your neighbors are all planning expanded gardens this year, and each of you needs to use a good rototiller. Rather than each of you laying out money to rent or purchase one, consider going in on it together. If the daily rental fee of a tiller is, say, $75, you each chip in $25 and work as a team to get all three gardens done in one day.

Sounding boards: While knowledge of good-quality survival-related websites, social media groups, and YouTube channels is certainly advisable, it's always great to pick the brains of folks who are intimately familiar with your local area. If you were looking for a great romantic restaurant to celebrate your anniversary, would you have better luck using Google or asking around at work?

Barter/trade: When circumstances prevent you from running to the hardware store to get the tool you need to fix your generator, you may find that a neighbor has exactly what you need. He'll help you get the generator fixed, and in turn you'll let him charge up a few batteries. Or perhaps he's drowning in eggs and would love to trade you a dozen if you happen to have a pound of flour or sugar. Maybe he can help you fix that leak in your roof if you could help weed his garden. Back in the day, folks did these sorts of things all the time.

Security: The more eyes and ears paying attention to what happens in the neighborhood, the better as far as I'm concerned. Granted, every neighborhood has a "busybody" who feels it's a calling to know just who is sleeping with whom and where, and those folks are at times a bit hard to handle. But they're the same ones who'll be able to tell you just how many times that navy blue SUV has driven through the neighborhood late at night.

It can be difficult, though, to make a connection when it comes to prepping. Often, we feel that we'll be ridiculed or mocked for our interest in planning for a calamity. But given the rapid increase in both interest in and awareness of prepping—look at the numerous TV shows, books, and websites discussing it—I think things are changing, at least a bit. More and more people are waking up to the reality that they need to prepare themselves and their families, rather than rely on a government agency to swoop in and save the day.

I'm not suggesting that you go door-to-door in your area, asking if people have heard the end is nigh and inviting them over for a tour of your preps. What I am suggesting is bringing up the subject of prepping with your neighbors to gauge their interest. Could be they just saw an episode of *The Walking Dead* or a similar show or movie and they're interested in learning how to prepare for more realistic sorts of disasters.

Lately, I've been fielding emails and messages from family and friends who are suddenly interested in learning more about prepping. Sometimes it's the result of a TV show or book; other times it's like the blinders just fell off and common sense has returned. Whatever the case is, I'm always happy to answer any questions they have. You should do the same.

WEEK 19 ASSIGNMENTS

TASKS

☐ Make contact with at least three people this week and work the subject of prepping into the conversation. I don't care if they're immediate neighbors, coworkers, or local family members. Consider using recent news stories about stranded motorists as a starting point. Talk about vehicle emergency kits, bug out bags, that sort of stuff to get the ball rolling.

☐ Review previous assignments and complete those that are unfinished.

SAVINGS

☐ Add $10 to your Prepper Savings Account.

Total Prepper Savings Account: ☐

WATER STORAGE

☐ Store 1 gallon (or two 2-liter bottles) of water per person or a case of bottled water for the household.

Total Water Storage: ☐

GROCERY LIST

☐ 3 cans vegetables, your choice

☐ 2 cans fruit, your choice, but stick with those packed in water or juice, rather than syrup

☐ 2 cans meat (tuna, chicken, beef), your choice

☐ 2 cans soup, not condensed (they require water)

☐ 1 package dry soup mix, your choice

☐ 1 pound pasta, your choice

☐ **WEEK COMPLETED**

Date:_____

WEEK 20
MAKING FIRE

While *Countdown to Preparedness* is more about things like sheltering in place and bugging out, wilderness survival skills are also part of an overall disaster readiness plan. Learning and becoming adept at such skills is great for increasing your self-confidence. Making a fire, building a temporary shelter, and navigating your way back to safety from the middle of the forest are all basic, yet necessary, skills.

Being able to get a fire going is crucial to survival. Fire will keep you warm, cook your food, light up the night, and generally provide comfort in a stressful situation. There's little else that can give peace and serenity like an evening spent watching a campfire.

Of course, we have devised many ways to start a fire. Disposable lighters, ferrocerium rods, matches, flint, and steel, the list goes on and on. But all those tools boil down to the same thing—providing the spark to get the tinder lit. Really, that's the easy part. Keeping the fire from dying out is harder.

Tinder consists of dry, easy-to-light material. Cotton balls, dryer lint, and paper all qualify. There are many natural sources as well, such as dried grass. The tinder should be material that will catch and hold a spark and burn long enough to start your kindling going.

Kindling consists of small sticks, at most about as big around as your finger. They should be dry and brittle. The drier they are, the easier it is to get them burning.

The idea here is to start small and work your way up. Tinder gets the kindling going. Kindling gets the larger twigs going. The larger twigs get the thicker logs burning, and so on. You can't rush this process. Doing so will result in you having to start over. By adding too much fuel too quickly, you'll smother the flames.

Clear a spot in your backyard to practice making campfires. Use your common sense here and don't set up next to your wood privacy fence. Scrape the spot down to bare dirt. If you have one of those patio fireplaces, use that if you'd like. Gather a couple of armfuls of sticks as well as a couple of handfuls of tinder. Make a small teepee with the sticks and place the tinder inside. What you're hoping to do is get the tinder lit and have it burn up through the teepee, getting the sticks burning. When the teepee collapses, you can slowly add more fuel.

While this is only one of many ways to build a campfire, I've found most people are successful with this method even without practice.

Once you have a small fire going, add larger sticks a little at a time to build it up as needed. You may be surprised at how small the fire can be and still warm you up on a chilly night.

This is a basic skill, and many of you probably mastered it long ago. But I'm sure you'll all agree it's an essential one and should be practiced until you're proficient at it.

WEEK 20 ASSIGNMENTS

TASKS

❏ Practice making campfires. Use different methods to light the fire and different materials for tinder. See what works best for you and what doesn't.

❏ If you don't have these items already, add them to your shopping list for the week: disposable lighters (BIC, Clipper, or Scripto preferred; avoid cheap generics), ferrocerium rods, and storm matches. For those interested in more primitive means of fire making, do some independent homework on bow drills and the like.

SAVINGS

❏ Add $15 to your Prepper Savings Account.

Total Prepper Savings Account: _____

WATER STORAGE

❏ Store 1 gallon (or two 2-liter bottles) of water per person or a case of bottled water for the household.

Total Water Storage: _____

GROCERY LIST

❏ 3 cans vegetables, your choice

❏ 2 cans fruit, your choice, but stick with those packed in water or juice, rather than syrup

❏ 1 can chili or stew, your choice

❏ 1 package or jar gravy, your choice

❏ 1 pound white rice

❏ **WEEK COMPLETED**

Date:_____

WEEK 21
ENTERTAINMENT

In the wake of many types of emergencies, you may end up with time on your hands. Without power, you won't have ready access to television or the internet to distract you. Sure, you may be spending more time than usual with meal preparation and other chores, as well as possibly cleaning up from the disaster (downed trees and such), but remember, even the pioneers had some downtime.

It's a good idea to think about how you and your family can spend those hours, rather than endure endless circular conversations centered on "I don't know, what do you want to do?"

Board games are something almost everyone has stashed in a closet or cupboard. But does *Clue* still have all the pieces? Go through the games and make sure everything needed is there. Replacement pieces are something you can pick up for spare change at rummage sales and thrift stores.

There are a ton of different games you can play with decks of cards, too. You can stock up on several decks for just a couple of bucks. It isn't the worst idea to pick up a book on card games, to learn at least one or two games that are new to you and the family.

Dice can also be used to play several different games, both by yourself and as a group. By having a few sets on hand, you have the bonus of being able to use them with the board games if you lose the dice from the game. As with the cards, there are books available that explain the rules for many different games.

My wife and I are both voracious readers so, naturally, we have a house full of books. While recreational reading isn't everyone's cup of tea, if you or members of your family enjoy the solitude of digging into a tale of intrigue, romance, or adventure, stock up on reading material. You can also have family reading time, when you each take turns reading sections of a book out loud. You'll find interesting books at rummage sales, thrift stores, and library sales, often for less than a dollar a book.

Especially for the younger family members, arts and crafts can help the hours fly by. You can find construction paper, scissors, glue, glitter, and other tools of the trade on sale during back-to-school season. If you bring out a box of these goodies, children's eyes are sure to light up. Toss in a couple of notebooks and pens for the older children (or adults) to keep journals about their experiences during the crisis. Not only does this help time go by, but it can be valuable psychologically to get thoughts down on paper to help with healing emotional trauma or stress.

If you or family members have musical abilities, an evening or two could be spent playing instruments and singing. You might never reach Partridge Family skill level, but as long as you have fun with it, that's what matters.

Boredom can actually be rather stressful. We live in such a go, go, go society that sitting still and doing nothing feels somehow wrong. While there's certainly something to be said for quiet contemplation, even meditation, that's hard to accomplish when every five minutes you have someone whining, "I'm bored!"

WEEK 21 ASSIGNMENTS

TASKS

☐ Take a look around the house and see what you might already have on hand for boredom killers. Check the board games and ensure that all the pieces are present and accounted for. Consider picking up a few other games or the supplies for some of the other suggestions listed above.

SAVINGS

☐ Add $10 to your Prepper Savings Account.

Total Prepper Savings Account: ☐

WATER STORAGE

☐ Store 1 gallon (or two 2-liter bottles) of water per person or a case of bottled water for the household.

Total Water Storage: ☐

GROCERY LIST

☐ 3 cans vegetables, your choice
☐ 2 cans fruit, your choice, but stick with those packed in water or juice, rather than syrup
☐ 1 package nuts, dried fruit, or trail mix
☐ 1 treat, such as a bag of popcorn, a bag of hard candy, or chocolate bars
☐ 1 gallon cooking oil (vegetable oil is preferred, for longer shelf life)

☐ **WEEK COMPLETED**

Date:_____

SECTION III
SUMMER

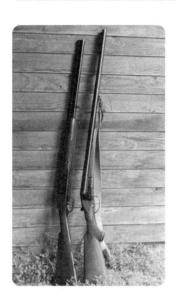

WEEK 22
FIREARMS

While I feel some survivalists and preppers overcompensate in this category, firearms are indeed necessary to a well-rounded disaster readiness plan. They serve two purposes: self-defense and food procurement.

Many of us would love to be able to afford a room full of semiautomatic rifles and military-style shotguns, but the reality is that firearms are expensive and ammo ain't cheap either. And if you're relatively new to firearms, you're going to burn through a lot of ammo before you become proficient.

Your first investment should be a .22 long rifle (LR). The Ruger 10/22 is just about the best there is in this category. A .22 LR rifle is great for small-game hunting as well as just practicing marksmanship. Ammo isn't quite as cheap and plentiful as it was in years past, but it can still be acquired if you hunt around for it. Of course, there are all sorts of add-ons and customizations you can do to the rifle to make it look cool and mean. But all that stuff is just cosmetic.

Next is the 12-gauge shotgun. With an enormous range in shell types, a shotgun is very versatile. From big game to waterfowl hunting, it'll keep your kettle full. A shotgun makes a good defensive weapon. What it lacks in long range, it makes up for in power.

Third is a hunting rifle. This is your long-range weapon. An AR-style rifle is a good option. They are commonly available, and the ammunition isn't scarce. There are any number of accessories for them, if you feel the need to customize the firearm. Make sure you have at least a few magazines for each rifle.

Next on the list is a handgun. They come in two flavors. Revolvers typically have a six-shot cylinder, though that can vary a bit depending on the model and caliber. Semiautomatics have a magazine and typically have a capacity of nine or more. If for no other reason than capacity, semiautos are preferred over revolvers for defense purposes. And that's exactly what a handgun is for, personal defense.

The choice of a specific firearm is a personal one. It depends on budget as well as physicality. Someone with small hands may not feel comfortable handling and using a large-caliber handgun, for example.

As you begin acquiring firearms, safety is paramount. Be sure to have a secure location to keep them locked up and away from kids. Many sheriff's departments offer trigger locks for free, so start with those if you can't afford a gun safe. Ammo should be locked up securely as well.

You'll also need to learn how to care for the firearms. Have someone teach you how to disassemble and clean each weapon. You may be able to find a class through a local shooting range. If nothing else, they might be able to refer you to a private instructor. There are also instructional videos available online for virtually any firearm. Stock up on cleaning supplies, as well as spare parts for each weapon.

Of course, all the firearms in the world won't do you much good if you don't know how to shoot straight. Make it a priority to practice with your firearms regularly. If you don't have a friend or relative who is proficient with shooting, inquire about classes at your local gun ranges. Odds are you can find someone who's willing to give you the help you may need. Accuracy takes time to achieve, and it's a skill that's lost over time if you don't practice.

WEEK 22 ASSIGNMENTS

TASKS

☐ If you've already completed at least one section in this book, and you've been able to contribute the specified amounts to your Prepper Savings Account, you should have a tidy little nest egg to use for shopping for a firearm. If you still lack the funds to do so, begin setting aside your nickels and dimes as best you can. For those new to firearms, consider purchasing a .22 LR as your first one, then branch out from there.

☐ Locate a range in your area where you can practice shooting as well as receive instruction if needed.

SAVINGS

☐ You're spending this week, not saving. Use your savings to pick up a firearm and ammunition.

Total Prepper Savings Account: _____

WATER STORAGE

☐ Store 1 gallon (or two 2-liter bottles) of water per person or a case of bottled water for the household.

Total Water Storage: _____

GROCERY LIST

☐ 3 cans vegetables, your choice
☐ 2 cans fruit, your choice, but stick with those packed in water or juice, rather than syrup
☐ 2 cans meat (tuna, chicken, beef), your choice
☐ 2 cans soup, not condensed (they require water)
☐ 1 canister oatmeal or 1 box flavored instant oatmeal
☐ 1 box granola bars, protein bars, or equivalent
☐ 1 canister table salt
☐ 1 pound white rice

☐ **WEEK COMPLETED**

Date:_____

WEEK 23
ALTERNATE MODES OF TRANSPORTATION

In many types of disasters, cars and trucks may not be your best bet for transportation. After a major event like a tornado or flood, roads may be all but impassable. Add to that a lack of readily available fuel, and most folks are going to be hoofing it to get anywhere.

Plan ahead for this possibility. In many cases, a bicycle will serve your needs well. You can pick them up cheap at rummage sales. Some of them may need a little TLC to be roadworthy again, but repairing a bicycle is not rocket science. Remember, we're not talking about expensive racing bikes here. A few simple mountain bikes will do nicely.

For about $30, you can get all the stuff you need to keep a bike on the road. Make sure you pick up tube repair kits as well as extra tubes. Get a small bag that will hang under the seat or over the handlebars to store wrenches, tubes, a small bottle of WD-40, pliers, and other odds and ends. Pick up a bike pump designed to fit on the bike frame when not in use.

Remember that, in some cases, the bike might be more useful for carrying cargo than carrying you. This was a lesson learned in many third world countries. A bike can carry a whole lot in bags and items lashed to the frame, with you pushing it. That's far easier than trying to carry all that stuff on your back.

If you keep your eyes open, you can often find a trailer for the bike rather cheap. Look for one designed to carry one or two children as well as convert to a stroller. These mount on the rear of the bike easily and will handle bigger loads. After all, they're made to carry a couple of kids. The stroller conversion can be handy if you reach a point where you'll have to ditch the bike for some reason.

Don't forget a lock. I like to use combination locks, so I don't have to worry about losing the key.

Of course, horses are another time-honored method of transportation. But they're much more expensive than bicycles and require a lot of upkeep. I'm told that hay has skyrocketed in price in recent years. But if you have the means to have a few horses, as well as the knowledge to take care of them, they're certainly a viable option. And packhorses can carry quite a bit of gear and supplies.

Motorcycles are also an option. They run on far less fuel than a car or truck. But they do require some training on how to operate them, as well as the requisite license. While you'd think law enforcement would have better things to do in the aftermath of a disaster than look for unlicensed motorcyclists, don't push your luck.

Given that the odds are great that no matter what you have planned for transportation you'll still likely end up on foot at some point, I encourage you to go for daily walks if at all possible. Start small if need be. Even going around the block once is better than nothing. Gradually increase the distance as your health and physical condition allow. Get used to putting one foot in front of the other as a way to get to where you're going.

WEEK 23 ASSIGNMENTS

TASKS

❏ Determine which alternate modes of transportation are viable for you in your particular situation. If you decide bicycles are the way to go, acquire them as cheaply as you can and repair them as needed. If it's been a while since you last rode, get back in the saddle by going out regularly. The saying is true, y'know. You never really forget how to ride a bike.

❏ Take a look at your planned evacuation routes. Will any of them need to be altered if you're not able to use a motor vehicle?

SAVINGS

❏ Add $10 to your Prepper Savings Account.

Total Prepper Savings Account: ⬚

WATER STORAGE

❏ Store 1 gallon (or two 2-liter bottles) of water per person or a case of bottled water for the household.

Total Water Storage: ⬚

GROCERY LIST

- ❏ 3 cans vegetables, your choice
- ❏ 2 cans fruit, your choice, but stick with those packed in water or juice, rather than syrup
- ❏ 1 can chili or stew, your choice
- ❏ 1 package or jar gravy, your choice
- ❏ 1 jar peanut butter (if allergies are an issue, choose an allergen-free version, such as sunflower butter)
- ❏ 1 jar pasta sauce, your choice
- ❏ 1 jar honey (100 percent real honey, not flavored corn syrup)
- ❏ 1 pound dry beans, your choice

❏ **WEEK COMPLETED**

Date:_____

WEEK 24
PREPARING FOOD OFF-GRID

While I've discussed the need to stockpile foods that require little or no preparation before consuming, during an extended emergency, you'll want to be able to cook. But if the utility services have been interrupted, your microwave and stovetop may not be particularly useful.

A hot meal is comforting, and having the means to cook food opens up more possibilities for meals. And, as I discussed in the lesson on water filtration and purification, boiling water is one of the best ways to prevent the ingestion of bacteria and other harmful organisms.

You can use several methods to cook food when the power is off.

Grills: Whether propane or charcoal, grills need not be limited to just cooking meat. Of course, many propane grills today are equipped with side burners designed for use with pots and pans. But even without that feature, you can simply place your pot on the grill to heat it up. I was talking to a woman a couple of years back who had suffered through a severe ice storm that knocked out power for several days. She lamented that while her family had a charcoal grill, there weren't any briquettes for it, so in her eyes, it was worthless. I pointed out that she could have just used small pieces of firewood, a thought that had never occurred to her.

If you don't already own a grill, consider investing in one. Charcoal ones in particular can be had fairly cheap if you shop around. Check Facebook Marketplace for used ones. Don't forget to pick up long-handled utensils as well. Your fingers will thank you.

Decorative firepits: These have become popular in the last few years. Usually made of metal, these portable firepits can sit on your patio to keep you warm on chilly nights. They pretty much amount to portable campfires, and people have been cooking over an open flame for almost as long as there have been people.

Campfires: If nothing else, you can cook over a small campfire in your backyard. Clear a spot away from your house and outbuildings and keep a stash of firewood nearby.

When using any sort of campfire setup, remember that the best way to cook is to use the coals, rather than a roaring fire. The coals give off a higher, steadier heat.

While you can use your normal pots and pans if that's all you have, they aren't designed for campfire cooking. They're likely to warp under the high heat. Shop around for cast-iron cooking implements. To start, get a good-sized frying pan and a Dutch oven. These two items will serve you well in preparing just about anything.

If you're not familiar with cooking over an open flame or coals, it does take some practice. This isn't something you'll pick up overnight. It is just as much an art form as it is a way to prepare a meal. These aren't skills that you can learn from reading a few books. You need to get out there and practice.

Solar ovens: If you hit up Google for "DIY solar oven," you'll get umpteen thousand hits. They're fairly simple to construct from common materials and work well during daylight hours. Again, there's a learning curve for using these ovens. Don't wait until they're truly needed before you put one together and see how it works.

Camp stoves: These can be found in any decent sporting goods store. They're little stove tops that usually use small gas cylinders for fuel, though there are a wide range of models and designs. These generally work very well and store in a small space. I see them fairly often at yard sales, usually from families who decided they didn't like camping all that much.

Please remember, with the exception of small camp stoves, these methods of using any sort of open flame for cooking should never be used inside the home. There's a danger of fire as well as carbon monoxide poisoning.

WEEK 24 ASSIGNMENTS

TASKS

☐ Select a couple of ways to cook food without using your normal kitchen appliances and begin acquiring the necessary items.

☐ If a charcoal grill is on your list, begin picking up bags of charcoal when it goes on sale. If propane is more your style, make sure you have at least a couple of filled tanks as backup.

☐ Get outside this week and cook a meal outside. I mean the whole meal, not just the main course. Pretend the kitchen cooking appliances are off-limits. You may just learn you like the taste of this sort of meal better than anything that comes out of a microwave.

SAVINGS

☐ Add $15 to your Prepper Savings Account.

Total Prepper Savings Account: ☐

WATER STORAGE

☐ Store 1 gallon (or two 2-liter bottles) of water per person or a case of bottled water for the household.

Total Water Storage: ☐

GROCERY LIST

☐ 3 cans vegetables, your choice.
☐ 2 cans fruit, your choice, but stick with those packed in water or juice, rather than syrup
☐ 2 cans meat (tuna, chicken, beef), your choice
☐ 2 cans soup, not condensed (they require water)
☐ 1 jar jelly or fruit preserves
☐ 1 box (12 packages) ramen noodles
☐ 1 sack cornmeal
☐ 1 pound pasta, your choice

☐ **WEEK COMPLETED**

Date:_____

WEEK 25
HIDDEN STORAGE

Whether it's silver coins, ammunition, or food, there are likely things you'd like to keep hidden from prying eyes. You certainly don't want your valuables ending up in someone else's possession if the house is searched or looted.

Fortunately, many places inside the home are easy to convert into covert stashes. Let's start at the bottom and work our way up.

The basement is full of great hiding places. Ventilation ducts work well, as long as what you're hiding won't be adversely affected by heat or cold. Look for the vents that are on the side of the duct, open them up, and place your stuff inside. Be careful to not obstruct too much of the air flow, though.

If you look at the basement ceiling, you should find at least one run of large-diameter PVC pipe. This is for waste coming out of the bathroom. You could easily hang another run of this pipe somewhere else in the basement without it looking out of place. Try to match the same color of PVC, as well as the hanging hardware, to what's already there. These pipes are large enough to use for storing extra ammunition, perhaps even a rifle.

Another option, and about as cheap and easy as it gets, is to fill a few cardboard boxes with your good stuff, then label them as "Grannie's old clothes" or something along those lines. You could even take the extra step of placing some thrift store clothing at the top of the box, in case someone peeks inside. If you want to be even sneakier, use a specific color marker to label the "special" boxes, so you can know at a glance which ones to grab when needed.

Moving up to the main level, you can install a few additional baseboard vents in a room or two. Line up the vent along the wall so you know the dimensions, then cut away the wall, exposing the space between the studs. Put in a brick or two of ammunition, then screw down the vent. For quicker access, instead of screws you could use two-face tape or magnets.

Instead of a baseboard vent, you could just leave the wall open and hide the hole with a small bookcase or other piece of furniture. This, however, makes rearranging furniture later rather interesting.

There's often empty space inside closets, just above the door. This can be a great place for a shelf. While not as hidden as other places, few people think to look there. While you're looking in the closets, if you have a fair amount of DIY ability, you could even create a false back to the closet. Frame in the space, put up drywall, and no one will be the wiser.

Slim items, like paper currency or coins, can be hidden inside photo frames. Tape the items to the back of the photo or the inside of the back plate, then replace it in the frame. Who really wants to steal your wedding pictures? Just don't use frames that look valuable.

Bags of pet food, birdseed, or water softener pellets are all good places to stash some goodies. Freezers are another location, inside containers labeled cow tongue or perhaps pig feet.

If you have easy access to the attic, this is another place to consider. It bears noting, though, that this space is often subject to extremes of heat and cold, so avoid hiding anything perishable or temperature sensitive there. You can just bury items inside the insulation. Just be careful you don't do this with anything heavy enough to fall through the ceiling.

WEEK 25 ASSIGNMENTS

TASKS

☐ Explore your own options for hidden storage and begin implementing them. Use these techniques to keep your goodies safe from prying eyes and fingers.

☐ Revisit previous lessons and complete any unfinished assignments.

SAVINGS

☐ Add $10 to your Prepper Savings Account.

Total Prepper Savings Account: _____

WATER STORAGE

☐ Store 1 gallon (or two 2-liter bottles) of water per person or a case of bottled water for the household.

Total Water Storage: _____

GROCERY LIST

☐ 3 cans vegetables, your choice

☐ 2 cans fruit, your choice, but stick with those packed in water or juice, rather than syrup

☐ 1 can chili or stew, your choice

☐ 1 package or jar gravy, your choice

☐ 1 box baking mix, preferably the type that doesn't require eggs, milk, or other ingredients

☐ 1 pound white rice

☐ **WEEK COMPLETED**

Date:_____

WEEK 26
HAND TOOLS

Two common elements of most moderate to severe disasters are the following:

1. No electricity will be available.

2. Immediate repairs and debris removal will have to be done by you.

While improvising is the hallmark of any good prepper, whenever possible you should use the right tool for the job. Naturally, it's difficult to do that if your tools consist of a butter knife for a screwdriver and a rock for a hammer. Having a cordless drill is a great idea, but without power it'll be difficult to charge the battery. Below are lists of the basic tools everyone should have.

BASIC TOOLS

- ☐ Hammer
- ☐ Bow saw
- ☐ Set of wrenches (SAE and metric)
- ☐ Channel lock pliers
- ☐ Screwdriver set (slotted and Phillips)
- ☐ Duct tape
- ☐ WD-40 or equivalent
- ☐ Pry bar
- ☐ Wire cutters
- ☐ Electrical tape

These basics will take care of most simple repair work as well as help you remove brush and the like if need be. A collection of nails and screws will also be useful for many jobs.

Once the basics are taken care of, you can move on to the intermediate level. These are tools that, while not critical, make many jobs easier.

INTERMEDIATE-LEVEL TOOLS

- ❏ Socket set (SAE and metric)
- ❏ Needle-nose pliers
- ❏ Hacksaw (with extra blades)
- ❏ Extendable magnet (great for picking up dropped screws and nails)
- ❏ Loppers
- ❏ Sledgehammer
- ❏ Crowbar
- ❏ More duct tape (honestly, you can never have enough)
- ❏ Come-along

Safety is always important, but during and after a disaster, it becomes even more critical. Make sure you have safety equipment like heavy-duty work gloves and eye protection. Thick-soled work boots are important as well.

Tools like chain saws are, of course, excellent additions to the tool collection, as long as you have fuel, oil, and sharp chains.

The idea here isn't to amass an entire hardware store in your garage, though if you have the means to do so, more power to you! Instead, you'll want to put together a set of basic hand tools that will help you with any emergency repairs and also take care of blown-down trees, branches, and other debris.

You need not go out and purchase all these tools at once. But, with tools as much as anything else, you get what you pay for. A set of wrenches purchased at your local dollar store will likely bend all over the place the first time you try to loosen a stubborn bolt or nut. I'm all about buying on the cheap when possible, but tools are not the place to get stingy. Spend the money to get quality items.

Quite often, you can find inexpensive hand tools at rummage sales. Pick up a wrench here for a quarter, a couple of screwdrivers there for a dollar, and you'll soon have a decent set of tools without breaking the bank. I haven't had much luck finding tools at thrift stores, but your experience might be different. Watch for quality name brands like Craftsman and Stanley. Older tools in particular are usually well made. If they look rusty, that doesn't mean they're worthless. A little elbow grease, some WD-40, and a nylon scrubbing sponge and they'll likely clean up well and last you a lifetime if you take care of them.

WEEK 26 ASSIGNMENTS

TASKS

☐ Begin shopping around for your tools. If you already have the basics, look for gaps in your collection and work to fill them in.

☐ If you lack appropriate safety equipment, such as gloves, safety glasses, and work boots, it's time to acquire them.

SAVINGS

☐ Add $15 to your Prepper Savings Account.

Total Prepper Savings Account: _____

WATER STORAGE

☐ Store 1 gallon (or two 2-liter bottles) of water per person or a case of bottled water for the household.

Total Water Storage: _____

GROCERY LIST

☐ 3 cans vegetables, your choice
☐ 2 cans fruit, your choice, but stick with those packed in water or juice, rather than syrup
☐ 2 cans meat (tuna, chicken, beef), your choice
☐ 2 cans soup, not condensed (they require water)
☐ 1 jar instant coffee (even if you don't drink coffee, this is a great barter item)
☐ 1 package dry soup mix, your choice
☐ 1 pound dry beans, your choice

☐ **WEEK COMPLETED**

Date:_____

WEEK 27
SUGAR, SPICE, AND EVERYTHING NICE

One downside of many long-term storage foods is they're somewhat bland. Rice and beans will get boring after a while. Sure, you can add some rehydrated ground beef to change it up a bit, but still, rather blah.

While you can buy things like meals ready to eat (MRE) and other dehydrated or freeze-dried meals, they're expensive. A case or two set aside for short-term emergencies is a great idea, but you'll put quite a dent in your budget trying to stock up on enough to last a family of four or five for months on end.

I look at food storage as setting aside ingredients for meals, rather than meals themselves. Ingredients give you options. As any cook worth his or her salt will tell you, spices and herbs can make or break a meal.

Freshly caught fish is pretty good, but if you add salt, pepper, and maybe a bit of lemon pepper? Mmm, really good! Even better, use flour and some spices for a breading, then fry it up.

Spices are crucial to a long-term food storage plan. So are baking staples.

Here's a short list of herbs and spices that I consider essential.

HERBS AND SPICES

- ☐ Salt
- ☐ Ground pepper (or peppercorns with a grinder)
- ☐ Paprika
- ☐ Garlic powder
- ☐ Oregano
- ☐ Basil
- ☐ Cinnamon
- ☐ Chili powder
- ☐ Cayenne pepper
- ☐ Bay leaves (not really a spice, but along the same lines)
- ☐ Curry powder
- ☐ Nutmeg
- ☐ Crushed red pepper
- ☐ Thyme
- ☐ Rosemary
- ☐ Nutmeg

BAKING ESSENTIALS

- ☐ Flour
- ☐ Sugar
- ☐ Powdered sugar
- ☐ Baking powder
- ☐ Vanilla extract
- ☐ Baking soda
- ☐ Cream of tartar
- ☐ Cocoa powder
- ☐ Oil and shortening (watch the expiration dates on these)
- ☐ Yeast

Naturally, the fresher the ingredients in a recipe, the better. But all the above will store reasonably well in cool, dark places. With access to those ingredients, coupled with basic food storage items like canned meats and dry pasta, anyone should be able to put together a pretty tasty meal . . . one that will beat the heck out of canned soup.

The more experience you have with scratch cooking, the better off you are. If you aren't that adept around the kitchen, invest time and energy into improving your skills. Find a few of the gazillion recipe websites that look good and give them a shot. Even better, pick up your own copy of one or two basic cookbooks, like the Betty Crocker cookbooks. They'll not only have all the recipes you need but are full of tips and information about the art of cooking.

Setting aside buckets of rice and beans is just the tip of the iceberg. You need to learn how to use those and other ingredients. Sure, a plate of plain beans and rice will fill a belly and provide needed calories. But day after day of that will result in appetite fatigue.

Growing your own herbs for cooking is ideal. This is a wonderful idea for those plants that thrive in your area. But picking up small jars of dried herbs as a backup is also essential.

Don't overlook condiments either. Hot sauce improves just about everything, doesn't it? Other basics include ketchup, mustard, and BBQ sauce.

WEEK 27 ASSIGNMENTS

TASKS

☐ If you don't already possess at least rudimentary scratch cooking skills, begin working on that this week. Pick a few recipes to make and get cracking. Bonus points if the recipes use things you already have in your food storage.

☐ Begin gathering spices and baking essentials. Watch the best-by dates on things like oil and shortening and make sure you use them up before they go bad.

SAVINGS

☐ Add $20 to your Prepper Savings Account.

Total Prepper Savings Account:

WATER STORAGE

☐ Store 1 gallon (or two 2-liter bottles) of water per person or a case of bottled water for the household.

Total Water Storage:

GROCERY LIST

☐ 3 cans vegetables, your choice

☐ 2 cans fruit, your choice, but stick with those packed in water or juice, rather than syrup

☐ 1 can chili or stew, your choice

☐ 1 package or jar gravy, your choice

☐ 1 box tea bags (even if you don't drink tea, this is an excellent barter item)

☐ 1 box granola bars, protein bars, or equivalent

☐ 1 pound pasta, your choice

☐ **WEEK COMPLETED**

Date:_____

WEEK 28
IMPROVISED WEAPONS

When I was much younger, I worked as a bartender in a tavern. We didn't have too much trouble with people getting rowdy, but every once in a while, we had to break up a fight or argument. I was always amazed at the guys who grabbed a pool stick as a weapon. Long, cumbersome, not much more than a really thin bat. I'd grab three or four balls off the pool table, knowing I could nail a guy in the head from relative safety fifteen feet away.

When it comes to violent conflict, whenever possible you want to keep distance between you and your assailant. In most cases, firearms are the weapon of choice. But there may well be times when you aren't able to get to a firearm or use it safely. For example, your opponent might be standing in front of your child's bedroom and a bullet might penetrate that room. It could also be that you're not allowed to legally own or possess firearms.

In any event, you're deluding yourself if you believe a firearm is or should be your only line of defense.

While some people recommend using a can of hair spray and a lighter to make an improvised flamethrower, this isn't nearly as good an idea as it might sound. First, the range is only a couple of feet. Second, people hit in the face with that aren't going to just drop to the floor. They'll run around yelling and screaming, all the while possibly lighting up your curtains and other flammable items in the room. It makes little sense to burn your house down while you're trying to protect it.

Pepper spray works well and is obviously made for self-defense. But it isn't something most folks have lying around. I would encourage you to invest in a few canisters and stage them throughout your house, just in case.

I hesitate to recommend Tasers for a couple of reasons. First, if the person is wearing heavy clothing, the probes may not make contact with skin, which renders the weapon ineffective. Second, you get only one shot. You miss, and that's it.

One thing I want you to do this week is to walk through your house with an eye for readily accessible improvised weapons. Kitchens, of course, are full of goodies like knives and cleavers. But what about your living room or your foyer?

Use your imagination here. Is the vase of flowers you keep on a table right near the front door light enough for you to grab and swing? Maybe you have a couple of nice, solid candlesticks on a coffee table in the living room.

You should also consider positioning weapons throughout your home. If you have kids, a baseball bat resting in a corner will probably not look out of place. Pepper spray, as mentioned previously, comes in small enough canisters to hide almost anywhere. Naturally, if you have youngsters, keep them in mind and place these weapons where they aren't accessible to children. A can of soda in an old tube sock will work great as an improvised blackjack or sap. Grab the loose end of the sock and swing it over your head at your attacker. A cue ball works even better if you have one available.

The takeaway here is to have defensive weapons available to you in every room of your home . . . just in case.

WEEK 28 ASSIGNMENTS

TASKS

☐ Go through your home and practice implementing improvised weapons you find throughout. It's important to practice using these weapons so you're familiar with their weight and how they can be used.

☐ If you come across any rooms where you cannot easily find any improvised weapons, position items accordingly. Lean a baseball bat in the corner. Find a nice-looking vase to put on an end table. Ideally, no matter what room you're in, you should have something you could use as a weapon within easy reach.

SAVINGS

☐ Add $15 to your Prepper Savings Account.

Total Prepper Savings Account: ☐

WATER STORAGE

☐ Store 1 gallon (or two 2-liter bottles) of water per person or a case of bottled water for the household.

Total Water Storage: ☐

GROCERY LIST

☐ 3 cans vegetables, your choice

☐ 2 cans fruit, your choice, but stick with those packed in water or juice, rather than syrup

☐ 2 cans meat (tuna, chicken, beef), your choice

☐ 2 cans soup, not condensed (they require water)

☐ 1 box crackers, your choice

☐ 1 jar pasta sauce, your choice

☐ 1 pound pasta, your choice

☐ **WEEK COMPLETED**

Date:_____

WEEK 29
HAM RADIO

Ham radio operators are a key component in survival communications. Quite often, they may be the only source of information during a disaster. Most ham operators are networked in with emergency responders and assist with communicating information between agencies and such.

Before we go any further, let's talk briefly about licensing. It's required by law that you have a license before you can broadcast on ham frequencies. There's an argument that says that during and after a catastrophe, enforcement officers won't be looking for unlicensed radio operators. While that may be true, proficiency with ham radio isn't something you can really pick up on the fly. You need practice to truly understand how it all works and how to get the best use of your equipment. That practice entails actually using your gear, which requires the license.

And there's another consideration. While most ham operators are exceedingly generous with their time and experience when it comes to helping someone new, they have little regard for unlicensed operators. Ham operators may be your single best link to reliable information during a major event, and you don't want to get on their bad side by broadcasting without a proper license.

Getting your license costs very little and just requires you to pass a test. There are tons of books and websites to help you study for the test. It used to be that one of the requirements was to memorize Morse code, but that's no longer necessary.

OK, back to ham radios.

Shortwave consists of the radio frequencies between 1.8 and 30 MHz. This includes AM and FM voice transmissions as well as single side band (SSB), data, television, and several others, even including transmissions from other countries. Ham radio is another one of these subsets of shortwave. Think of it like this—shortwave radios allow you to gather information, whereas ham radios allow you to engage in two-way communication with other operators.

A ham setup, sometimes called a rig, consists of a receiver and a transmitter, which are sometimes all one unit called a transceiver. Ideally, this rig should be somewhat mobile, with the ability to power it using a 12-volt DC battery, so it can be installed in a vehicle, and/or with a solar charge system. This way, you can take it with you should you need to vacate your home for some reason.

There are many inexpensive transceivers available, such as those sold by the company Baofeng. Configured properly, these will meet your basic needs. For a basic transceiver, you could pay as little as $50 and be in business. Of course, the sky is the limit. You may find yourself with an exciting new hobby and end up investing thousands of dollars in high-end gear.

Given the high number of clubs in the country, a quick online search should find a ham operator group in your immediate area. Find out when and where they meet, then go there and introduce yourself. These are the folks you want to get to know well. Odds are very good they have their own repeater system in place. Basically, the way ham radio works is you transmit on a frequency, and this transmission will go to a repeater. This tower then sends the transmission on down the line, and it hits other repeaters as needed, until it reaches the destination.

Ham radio is not as complicated as it seems. It doesn't take long for the average person to get the hang of things. But, as with anything else, it's better to learn the lessons now, when time isn't a factor.

WEEK 29 ASSIGNMENTS

TASKS

☐ Find a local ham radio club in your area. Search "[county name] ham radio" online, and that should point you in the right direction. Contact the club and explain you're interested in getting involved with ham radio. I think you'll find members who will bend over backward to help you.

☐ Begin shopping around for a starter rig. Ask members of your local club for recommendations.

☐ Look for study materials online and study for and pass the license exam (no, I don't expect you to do that all in one week, but get it done ASAP).

SAVINGS

☐ Add $10 to your Prepper Savings Account.

Total Prepper Savings Account: _____

WATER STORAGE

☐ Store 1 gallon (or two 2-liter bottles) of water per person or a case of bottled water for the household.

Total Water Storage: _____

GROCERY LIST

☐ 3 cans vegetables, your choice
☐ 2 cans fruit, your choice, but stick with those packed in water or juice, rather than syrup
☐ 1 can chili or stew, your choice
☐ 1 package or jar gravy, your choice
☐ 1 box powdered milk
☐ 1 box (12 packages) ramen noodles
☐ 1 pound white rice

☐ **WEEK COMPLETED**

Date:_____

WEEK 30
SAFETY EQUIPMENT

The emergencies for which we prepare aren't always of the total societal collapse variety. Even if a disaster isn't global, or even regional, it can still be the end of the world as you know it, so to speak.

Imagine losing your entire home to a fire.

Or a member of your family dying from carbon monoxide poisoning.

Or the loss of your household's income because the primary wage earner was severely injured in an accident at home.

These things might not even affect your next-door neighbor but would be no less of a disaster for you and your family.

It's important to take the steps necessary to protect your family from relatively common emergencies. For starters, each level of your home should be outfitted with smoke detectors. They should be in good working order and tested every six months. When you test them, make sure you can actually hear one of the smoke detectors from inside your bedroom with the door closed.

While we're on the subject of fires, have you devised and practiced an evacuation plan? Each member of your family should know exactly what to do in the event of a fire. How should they leave the home, and where do they go?

Have a good-quality fire extinguisher in the kitchen, which is where many home fires start. It's important to know how to use one properly, so get in touch with your local fire department for guidance. They may

offer to show you with a hands-on demonstration. The acronym **PASS** can help remind you of the steps to follow:
- **P**ull the pin.
- **A**im the nozzle at the base of the fire.
- **S**queeze the handle.
- **S**weep the nozzle back and forth.

Each bedroom should have at least one working flashlight. This can be difficult to accomplish when you have smaller children, who will look at it as a toy. Do the best you can to stress to them the importance of having a working flashlight in case of emergencies. A good option for kids' bedrooms is a dynamo-powered flashlight. These have a crank handle that's wound several times to generate power. This means the light won't run out of battery power. Each bedroom should also have a small air horn, though use your best judgment on this if there are small children in the house. If someone's trapped in the room, the sound of that horn will be much louder than just a shout.

Carbon monoxide (CO) detectors are critical if you have fuel-burning appliances. Position them near your furnace and any other potential sources of CO in your home.

When you're working on projects, be sure to wear the proper safety gear. I'm one of those people who hates wearing ear plugs and safety glasses. But I do recognize the need for them and do give in from time to time when my wife badgers me. Heavy-duty work gloves should be worn to handle brush and other debris to avoid splinters, punctures, and other not-so-fun injuries.

If you don't have any, consider buying a pair of steel-toed work boots for at least the adults in the family. You can sometimes find them used at thrift stores. I wear mine all the time when working in the garage or around the house.

Masks should be worn anytime you're dealing with dust and airborne debris as well as fumes. N95 masks are ideal, and they're also useful to prevent germs from entering your body through the nose or mouth. Consider adding a few to each bedroom to help with smoke inhalation if there's a house fire.

When using ladders, be careful to not overextend your reach. Ensure the ladder is on a solid, level surface. If at all possible, have a spotter in case you do fall. That person won't necessarily catch you, but he or she can get help if needed.

Read all instructions for any power tools and be sure you totally understand how they're properly used. Rushing a job is just asking for trouble.

WEEK 30 ASSIGNMENTS

TASKS

☐ Test all smoke and CO detectors. Replace batteries as needed.

☐ If you don't have them already, invest in a few good-quality fire extinguishers.

☐ Start stocking up on and using the other safety gear mentioned above. Remember, the best gear in the world won't help you if you don't use it.

SAVINGS

☐ Add $10 to your Prepper Savings Account.

Total Prepper Savings Account: ☐

WATER STORAGE

☐ Store 1 gallon (or two 2-liter bottles) of water per person or a case of bottled water for the household.

Total Water Storage: ☐

GROCERY LIST

☐ 3 cans vegetables, your choice

☐ 2 cans fruit, your choice, but stick with those packed in water or juice, rather than syrup

☐ 2 cans meat (tuna, chicken, beef), your choice

☐ 2 cans soup, not condensed (they require water)

☐ 1 treat, such as a bag of hard candy, chocolate bars, or a canister of hot cocoa mix (the type that mixes with water, not milk)

☐ 1 pound dry beans, your choice

☐ **WEEK COMPLETED**

Date:_____

WEEK 31
BLADES FOR SURVIVAL

They say that the best survival knife is the one you have with you at the time. While that's certainly true, I like to improve my odds by including a few different blades in my main kits.

A good-quality knife is probably the number one most important tool in a survival kit. With it, you can make just about anything you need. Without it, you're behind the proverbial eight ball. Sure, you can probably make do in a pinch, but having a good knife makes things so much easier.

In a true survival situation away from home, there are three types of blades to consider. The first is a small pocketknife. With a blade length of three inches or so, it's small enough to handle more intricate work. And keeping it in your pocket ensures that you have it with you at all times.

The second is a good-quality sheath knife. This one will serve as your primary tool with most chores that require a blade. This knife will typically have a blade length of about four or five inches. You'll use it to dress game, build shelters, cut firewood, and other such tasks.

The third is a machete-type blade. While your sheath knife can do much of what a machete will, the longer and heavier blade will work better on clearing brush as well as serve as a defense weapon if needed.

You could combine the latter two categories and carry a larger sheath knife. I bounce back and forth with that option. There are a couple of caveats about using a larger sheath knife:

- It can be awkward for some tasks. You might find the larger sheath knife just too big and the pocketknife too small for some things.

- Using your sheath knife to clear brush will dull the blade quicker. If it isn't high-quality, you could end up damaging the blade with nicks and such.

For my primary blades, I carry a few different knives in my kit.

Folding knives can have one or more blades, along with other features and onboard tools. You can't go wrong with some flavor of Swiss Army Knife from Victorinox. I like the Hiker model because it has a wood saw that works pretty well. Other recommendations for folding knives include these:

- 110 Folding Hunter from Buck Knives
- Mudbug from Smith & Sons Knives
- Livewire from Kershaw Knives
- Mongrel from Vehement Knives

I have several different sheath knives that I bounce between when I hit the trail. My current favorites include these:

- EXT-1 from Bark River Knives
- Republic from Cold Steel
- Ursus 45 from White River Knives
- South Pole from TRC Knives

Another approach is to combine the pocketknife and sheath knife and carry a smaller fixed blade instead of a folding knife. I tend to favor this approach quite often. For pocket-carry fixed-blade knives, I can recommend these:

- Model 1 from White River Knives
- Grunt 2.0 from Vehement Knives
- Field Scalpel from D. Tope Knives
- Huntsman from Edge Knife Works

Note that I've been a knife collector for about forty years now. Nobody truly needs that many different knives, let alone the several dozen more I have squirreled away.

I carry the Cold Steel Kukri for my machete. Honestly, you can't go wrong with Cold Steel products. I had originally bought one for my father-in-law several years ago and was so impressed with it that I got one for myself. It has a good weight to it, not so heavy that it wears you out but plenty of heft to get the job done.

When choosing a knife, you should look for a few things. First, for a folding knife, you want a knife with a solid pivot when you open and close it. The knife should snap open and snap closed. While I'll admit Swiss Army Knives lack these features, I recommend getting something with both a locking blade and the ability to be opened one-handed.

For the sheath knife, get something with a full tang, nothing less. The tang is the part of the blade that goes into the handle. A full tang means the blade is one solid piece of metal all the way through to the bottom of the handle. Notice that this precludes the use of the popular hollow-handle survival knives. There's a reason for that—with few exceptions, those "survival knives" are crap.

You want good-quality steel. I'm not overly fond of serrated or half-serrated blades. While I recognize their usefulness, I question how you'll be able to sharpen them in the field. Remember, you want your knife sharp at all times. A dull knife is more dangerous than a sharp one, as you'll need to apply more pressure to a cut, which increases the chances of a slip.

The handle should not be completely smooth but should have some texture to it. This helps you hang on to it when it gets wet. Remember, too, that you'll be using this knife a lot in the field, and it should be comfortable in your hand.

The sheath should be protective of the blade and be comfortable to wear for extended periods.

There's no need to go out and spend hundreds of dollars on a single knife, but this isn't a place to cheap out on one either. I know a few people who just buy cheap and toss the knife when it breaks or gives out. If I'm going to bet my life on a piece of gear, I want it to hold up.

WEEK 31 ASSIGNMENTS

TASKS

☐ Begin shopping around for a pocketknife and sheath knife. Purchase them as your budget allows, but don't linger too long on this. Remember, a good blade is the most important tool in your survival kit. If need be, pick up something inexpensive but sturdy and upgrade later as finances allow.

☐ Don't forget to pick up sharpening implements and learn how to use them properly to maintain the edge on your blades.

SAVINGS

☐ Add $15 to your Prepper Savings Account.

Total Prepper Savings Account:

WATER STORAGE

☐ Store 1 gallon (or two 2-liter bottles) of water per person or a case of bottled water for the household.

Total Water Storage:

GROCERY LIST

☐ 3 cans vegetables, your choice

☐ 2 cans fruit, your choice, but stick with those packed in water or juice, rather than syrup

☐ 1 can chili or stew, your choice

☐ 1 package or jar gravy, your choice

☐ 1 canister flavored drink mix, the type that has the sugar already added

☐ 1 package dry soup mix, your choice

☐ 1 pound pasta, your choice

☐ **WEEK COMPLETED**

Date:_____

SECTION IV
FALL

WEEK 32
EVERYDAY CARRY

Everyday carry, often referred to with the abbreviation EDC, refers to the gear you keep with you throughout the day. I look at EDC as having two layers. The first is what I keep on my body, such as in my pockets or on my belt. The other is what I keep in some sort of bag or pack that I keep nearby. When I worked outside the home, I always had a backpack or messenger bag of some sort that went everywhere I did. I used it to carry work materials, but I also kept some survival-specific gear in it as well.

Understand that EDC is a very personal thing. Sure, there are some categories in this area that are fairly universal, but how you fill that slot is entirely up to you.

When it comes to on-body EDC, these are items that are easy to carry without weighing you down too much. Here are some of the most common items you'll want to include as part of your on-body gear:

- **Knife**—Until the cell phone came along, this was probably the single-most commonly carried EDC item.
- **Defense weapon**—Make your own decision on what you want to carry in this regard.
- **Lighter**—Having an easy way to get a fire started could be important.
- **Pocket flashlight**—A decent one isn't expensive, and it's good to have during a power outage.
- **Tourniquet**—If you're going to carry a weapon, you should carry a tourniquet if not a full trauma kit.

I know several people who include a small notepad and a writing utensil. This isn't a bad idea, particularly if you're like me and find typing on a phone keypad to be an exercise in frustration due to large fingers and small keys.

You have to be careful about on-body EDC as the weight can add up quickly. It can get to the point that you want a belt and suspenders, just to make sure your pants don't end up around your ankles. This is why it's a good idea to add an off-body component to your EDC equipment. Let's face it, unless you work in law enforcement or you're Batman, you probably aren't going to be carrying a ton of stuff on your belt.

This doesn't need to involve any sort of large backpack. It depends on what exactly you decide to carry, of course. But for my own needs, everything can fit into a small messenger bag and still leave enough room for a laptop and other work items. Here's what I carry in my off-body EDC bag:

- **Power bank and cords**—I have a small pouch in my pack that contains a power bank, plus a charging cord and wall adapter. Between these options, I can charge my phone or tablet anywhere.
- **Fire kit**—In another small pouch, I keep a spare lighter, a ferrocerium rod and striker, and some tinder. Odds are remote that I'll need this, but it weighs very little.
- **First aid**—You don't need to include anything outlandish, just things for tackling small injuries, as well as some over-the-counter medications for things like upset stomach or headaches.
- **Tool kit**—I've always found most multi-tools too heavy to carry on my belt comfortably. But I definitely keep one in my bag. Depending on your line of work or plans for the day, there are any number of small tools you might add to your EDC bag.

You might consider adding a few hygiene items as well. Say you get called into a meeting unexpectedly right after you had pizza and garlic bread for lunch. It'd be nice to be able to quickly brush your teeth, right? A toothbrush, travel-size toothpaste, hairbrush or comb, hand sanitizer, and whatnot won't take up much space at all.

There are a few other nice-to-have items you might consider tossing into the mix:

- **Tweezers**—These are good for removing splinters as well as manipulating small screws and such.
- **Magnifying glass**—I've officially reached the age where I find myself taking photos of labels and enlarging them on my phone to be able to read them. A magnifying glass is handy in that regard, as well as for finding the aforementioned splinters and the like.
- **Duct tape**—This is always handy for any number of things. A full roll is way too big, so I take an old gift card and wrap a few feet of tape around it.
- **Extra cash**—I try to keep a few dollars in bills and coins for use in vending machines.

For most of us, our EDC loadout develops organically over time. We find ourselves needing a certain type of tool on a regular basis, so we start carrying it with us. Keep in mind that part of the goal of EDC is to make your life easier. If you find yourself struggling to carry it all, then by all means, pare down the load.

For your EDC bag or pack, I suggest looking at these companies:

- 5.11 Tactical (511tactical.com)
- Tuff Possum Gear (tuffpossumgear.com)
- KY Handcrafted (kyhandcrafted.com)
- PNWBUSHCRAFT (pnwbushcraft.com)

WEEK 32 ASSIGNMENTS

TASKS

☐ Think about what you keep in your pockets or otherwise on your body as you go about your day. Are there things you never use and could probably leave home? How about tools or other items that would be handy to have close at hand regularly? Consider adding them to your daily EDC equipment list.

☐ Put together a small EDC kit that you can keep with or near you as you go about your daily routine. Don't feel like you need to go out and purchase anything new specifically for this kit. Just use whatever you have around the house already, if possible. Adjust the kit's contents as needed.

SAVINGS

☐ Add $10 to your Prepper Savings Account.

Total Prepper Savings Account: [   ]

WATER STORAGE

☐ Store 1 gallon (or two 2-liter bottles) of water per person or a case of bottled water for the household.

Total Water Storage: [   ]

GROCERY LIST

☐ 3 cans vegetables, your choice
☐ 2 cans fruit, your choice, but stick with those packed in water or juice, rather than syrup
☐ 2 cans meat (tuna, chicken, beef), your choice
☐ 2 cans soup, not condensed (they require water)
☐ 1 canister oatmeal or 1 box flavored instant oatmeal
☐ 1 box granola bars, protein bars, or equivalent
☐ 1 sack (5 pounds) flour
☐ 1 pound white rice

☐ **WEEK COMPLETED**

Date: _____

WEEK 33
MASS-CASUALTY EVENTS

It's an unfortunate reality that we seem to be at risk for encountering bad actors any time we head out into public. Active shooters and other mass-casualty events are all too common. As part of a comprehensive preparedness plan, you need to take steps to protect yourself and your family in such cases.

Anytime you enter a business, such as a store, restaurant, or movie theater, make it a habit to identify at least two different egress points. Many of these will be clearly marked as emergency exits. However, think outside the box. It's likely that there are also escape routes that aren't as easily seen. For example, just about every restaurant will have a back door through the kitchen where they receive deliveries. Stores often have something similar in the stockroom at the back of the building.

Depending on which floor you're on, windows could be egress points in a pinch, even if using one requires you throwing a chair through it first. If the interior walls are typical drywall construction, you could potentially smash your way through to the next room, squeezing between the studs.

In an emergency, herd mentality often takes over. If people need to flee a building, the default setting, so to speak, is to head to the door through which they entered. As a few people run that way, more will follow instinctively. This can lead to a massive crowd crushing one another trying to squeeze through a narrow doorway. We've seen this happen time and again in various settings, including nightclubs that caught fire, and it invariably leads to high body counts.

The same approach applies to outdoor sites like concert venues. Know where you can go quickly if you hear shots fired or if some other emergency situation occurs. Depending on the layout, as well as the threat, heading directly to the stage might be your best bet. There are always egress points backstage.

Incidentally, dealing with an emergency situation in a public place is one of the reasons why I strongly advise people to carry a small flashlight with them when they leave the house. There are several reasons why the power in a building might shut down during an emergency. While buildings should have emergency lighting of some sort that kicks on, part of prepping is being ready to handle your own needs as best you can, right? Don't count on using your cell phone's flashlight app, either. You might be low on power, and you'll want to conserve it. A good-quality pocket flashlight isn't prohibitively expensive, and it'll work wonders when you find yourself in a dark hallway. There are a lot of great brands out there. I favor Streamlight.

The standard recommended protocol for dealing with an active shooter is run, hide, fight. Run means to get out of the area if at all possible. Don't worry about belongings, just grab your family and beat feet.

If escape isn't feasible, find somewhere to hide. The goal is to make it difficult for the shooter to see you or get to you. If possible, barricade doors and cover windows. Make sure cell phones are silenced. Avoid making noise and wait for help to arrive. While you're waiting, make a plan to fight, just in case.

You should understand the difference between cover and concealment. Cover is something that will provide some degree of protection from gunfire. A brick or cinder block wall, for example, can be considered cover. Hunkering down behind the engine end of a vehicle is decent cover, as are large trees. Concealment, on the other hand, merely hides you but may not provide anything in the way of protection. A standard interior wall made from drywall is a good example of this concealment concept.

Should push come to shove and you have to fight, do so with every ounce of your being. Make use of any improvised weapons you can find. If you have others with you, a coordinated surprise attack could prove successful. Whether you're alone or in a group, it's critical that you don't hold back. There can be no hesitation. As the saying goes, "Fight like you're the third monkey on the ramp to Noah's ark, and it's starting to rain."

When police officers arrive, follow their instructions to the letter. It's important to understand that they are likely operating on very minimal information. They are going to be on high alert, with adrenaline spiking their pulse rates. Everyone will be seen as a threat until proven otherwise, so keep your hands up and open. Don't just jump out of hiding and run toward them, as that might not lead to a positive outcome.

Nobody likes to imagine active shooters or similar events happening, but they're a very real risk. It's best to plan ahead, just in case.

WEEK 33 ASSIGNMENTS

TASKS

☐ Start working on identifying points of egress when you enter businesses and other public places. Look for escape routes that other people are likely to overlook.

☐ If you don't carry one already, purchase a pocket flashlight and keep it with you every time you leave the house. You might be surprised at how often you find yourself using it, such as for checking your car at night before you get into it.

SAVINGS

☐ Add $15 to your Prepper Savings Account.

Total Prepper Savings Account: _____

WATER STORAGE

☐ Store 1 gallon (or two 2-liter bottles) of water per person or a case of bottled water for the household.

Total Water Storage: _____

GROCERY LIST

☐ 3 cans vegetables, your choice
☐ 2 cans fruit, your choice, but stick with those packed in water or juice, rather than syrup
☐ 1 can chili or stew, your choice
☐ 1 package or jar gravy, your choice
☐ 1 jar peanut butter (if allergies are an issue, substitute an allergen-free version, such as sunflower butter)
☐ 1 jar pasta sauce, your choice
☐ 1 sack (4 pounds) sugar
☐ 1 pound pasta, your choice

☐ **WEEK COMPLETED**

Date:_____

WEEK 34

PLANNING TO REGROUP

Think about how much time each member of your family spends outside the home. Work, school, socializing—often it seems that the only time we're at home as a family is when we're all sleeping, if even then. The odds of disaster striking when one or more family members are out and about is much greater than it happening when everyone is all in one place.

This can lead to a tense and anxiety-filled situation. The thought of not knowing where your loved ones are, whether they're OK, will be extremely nerve-racking. Can they get home from where they are? What if you need to evacuate the home? Do they know where to find you?

Sit down and make plans now.

First, if you have school-age kids, determine who will pick up the kids from school. Make sure this is communicated clearly to every member of the family. You might also consider having a note placed in your child's school file indicating that in the event of an emergency, you will pick up the child at school, and he or she should not be placed on the bus to go home. If your child is old enough to be driving to school, talk to him or her about the importance of coming straight home in an emergency, rather than going out sightseeing.

Next, decide on a rallying point away from home. This is to be used in the event that you can't get to your home for some reason. Pick a specific location that every member of your family will know how to get to, such as a local restaurant or a relative's home on the other side of town. The first-choice destination is home, of course. The rallying point is the meeting point only if home can't be reached.

Third, pick a relative or friend who lives outside the area to act as a communication hub. Instruct each member of the family to call this person to fill him or her in on each person's location and status. Sometimes local phone systems get overwhelmed and calls won't go through, but by having a contact out of the area, you can still have a way to at least relay messages. Make sure you volunteer yourself to do the same for that person.

Another thing to keep in mind is that even if phone lines and cell towers are being swamped, text messages will often still get through. Email is another option, as is social media.

If you have a trusted neighbor who is normally home when everyone in your family is gone for the day, perhaps ask him or her to keep an eye on the house and let you know when family members are home safe.

Knowing who is supposed to do what will go a long way toward lessening panic and anxiety. Granted, parents will always worry until their child is safe in their arms. The idea here, though, is to make plans and communicate them to everyone involved, making sure each person knows exactly what he or she is supposed to do.

WEEK 34 ASSIGNMENTS

TASKS

☐ Draw up your plans for regrouping in an emergency. Talk about them in detail with everyone involved so there are no misunderstandings or miscommunications.

☐ If you have children in school, talk to school officials about their emergency plans. What are teachers and students expected to do during a disaster? What's the procedure for picking up your children during or immediately after a crisis?

SAVINGS

☐ Add $10 to your Prepper Savings Account.

Total Prepper Savings Account: [   ]

WATER STORAGE

☐ Store 1 gallon (or two 2-liter bottles) of water per person or a case of bottled water for the household.

Total Water Storage: [   ]

GROCERY LIST

☐ 3 cans vegetables, your choice

☐ 2 cans fruit, your choice, but stick with those packed in water or juice, rather than syrup

☐ 2 cans meat (tuna, chicken, beef), your choice

☐ 2 cans soup, not condensed (they require water)

☐ 1 jar jelly or fruit preserves

☐ 1 box (12 packages) ramen noodles

☐ 1 box instant potatoes

☐ 1 pound white rice

☐ **WEEK COMPLETED**

Date:_____

WEEK 35
NONFOOD PANTRY ITEMS

Along with the basic requirements like food, water, and medicine, there are various items you'll want to stock up on that aren't crucial to survival but will make life easier during a crisis.

Paper plates, cups, and bowls: Odds are good that you'll need to ration your water consumption. Not washing dishes every day will help save water. When meals are finished, the paper plates and such can be burned in your fireplace or woodstove. For that reason, I'd avoid the thicker foam-type items and stick to paper goods. While you could burn plastic utensils, it doesn't take much water at all to wash them. You could probably wash an entire meal's worth of utensils with not much more than a cup of water. Of course, this is something more for short-term emergencies like an extended power outage. I'm not advising you to stock up on enough paper plates to last a year or more. Be sure to watch for sales on these items, as their regular price is often ridiculously expensive.

Paper towels: The same water conservation principle applies here. While I prefer to use a cloth towel for most things, and save a tree here and there, in an extended emergency, you don't want piles of soiled dish towels lying around for days on end. Again, the used paper towels can be burned.

Toilet paper: Need I say more? There are many alternatives you can use in a pinch, but let's face it, most of 'em stink. Strive for at least a full month's worth of toilet paper on hand at all times.

Cleaning products: While most homes have at least a small supply of these items, it isn't a bad idea to set aside a stash, just in case. If the emergency is such that you and your family are confined to your home for several days, then keeping things clean will not only be a morale boost but help reduce the possibility of spreading germs. There's no need to go out and buy a couple of cases of Windex to set on the floor of your pantry, though. In fact, a bottle of vinegar will go a long way toward killing germs.

Hand sanitizer: If the water isn't running from the taps, place a bottle of this in or near the bathroom to allow you and your family to wash up after using the facilities.

Baby wipes: A cleaner you is a happier you. In the absence of baths or showers, these wipes can at least get a layer of grime off. They'll work for toilet paper as well.

Diapers, diaper cream, and crib bedding: If you have a baby in the family or are expecting one soon, stock up on extras of these sorts of items and set them aside for when you may need them. Be sure to rotate out the diapers as the child grows and replace them with the larger sizes.

Garbage bags: These have many uses, from makeshift rain ponchos to toilet liners. Try to have at least an extra box or two on hand.

As always, watch the sale ads and pick up extras of these items when the price is right. Don't feel you need to buy them all at once, unless you just won the lottery and have a pocketful of cash you're looking to burn.

WEEK 35 ASSIGNMENTS

TASKS

☐ Add these nonfood pantry items to your perpetual shopping list and pick them up as you can. Set them aside for when you'll need them. Most of these items don't have expiration dates and will keep for a long time if stored in a cool, dry place.

☐ If you haven't done so recently, head to your local library and find a book or two on the subject of wilderness survival skills. Choose one or two of those skills and practice them.

SAVINGS

☐ Add $15 to your Prepper Savings Account.

Total Prepper Savings Account: [   ]

WATER STORAGE

☐ Store 1 gallon (or two 2-liter bottles) of water per person or a case of bottled water for the household.

Total Water Storage: [   ]

GROCERY LIST

☐ 3 cans vegetables, your choice
☐ 2 cans fruit, your choice, but stick with those packed in water or juice, rather than syrup
☐ 1 can chili or stew, your choice
☐ 1 package or jar gravy, your choice
☐ 1 box baking mix, preferably the type that doesn't require eggs, milk, or other ingredients
☐ 1 package dry soup mix, your choice
☐ 1 bottle multivitamins
☐ 1 pound dry beans, your choice

☐ **WEEK COMPLETED**
Date:_____

WEEK 36

CRANK RADIOS AND POLICE SCANNERS

Communication is vital for overall preparedness. First, you need a way to receive news from the world around you. Second, you need to be able to communicate with your family and friends, as well as your prepper support group if you have one. This week, we concentrate on the first element and tackle the second one later.

We live in a time of instant communication. We routinely receive news from around the world in little more than a heartbeat. Thirty years ago, if I wanted to send a message to a friend in the UK, my choices were a very expensive phone call or a letter that could take a week or more to arrive. Today, I can send an email and receive a response in a matter of minutes. I can also log in to a chat room and enjoy instantaneous communication.

We tend to take such things for granted. In these uncertain times, that instant communication could come to a screeching halt for any number of reasons. We may not have the internet to provide us with news from around the country or even in our own towns. We may not even have local TV broadcasts.

Fortunately, there are some options available to us to get news. First, invest in a decent-quality crank radio. These types of portable radios can be powered by simply turning a crank for a few minutes. Often, they come with lights, sirens, and other doodads. The critical thing is the radio. Make sure the one you get can receive AM/FM as well as shortwave and National Oceanic and Atmospheric Administration (NOAA) weather broadcasts. Play around with it for a while so you fully understand how to tune in stations of interest to you. Even in the most dire recent disasters, there were radio broadcasts to listen to for up-to-date information. These vital pieces of equipment have come down in price and can be found at most retailers, such as Walmart and Target.

Once upon a time, I'd have recommended picking up a radio scanner as well. You can program them to receive the radio traffic in your area, such as chatter between police officers, rescue squads, fire departments, and other emergency personnel. However, in recent years more and more departments are moving to digital transmissions, and older radio scanners won't pick them up. You can get a digital radio scanner that will work, but they're fairly pricey.

In light of that, a better option is to install an app on your phone that allows you to listen to those radio transmissions. You'll need an online connection, but the apps work very well.

WEEK 36 ASSIGNMENTS

TASKS

☐ Begin shopping around for basic communication equipment, including a crank radio.

☐ If it's been a while since you last approached an extended family member or friend who's reluctant about prepping, consider doing so this week. Remember, the more people you convert to being prepared, the fewer who might end up knocking on your door during a crisis.

SAVINGS

☐ Add $15 to your Prepper Savings Account.

Total Prepper Savings Account:

WATER STORAGE

☐ Store 1 gallon (or two 2-liter bottles) of water per person or a case of bottled water for the household.

Total Water Storage:

GROCERY LIST

☐ 3 cans vegetables, your choice
☐ 2 cans fruit, your choice, but stick with those packed in water or juice, rather than syrup
☐ 2 cans meat (tuna, chicken, beef), your choice
☐ 2 cans soup, not condensed (they require water)
☐ 1 jar instant coffee (even if you don't drink coffee, this is an excellent barter item)
☐ 1 box granola bars, protein bars, or equivalent
☐ 1 treat, such as a bag of chips or popcorn, a bag of hard candy, or chocolate bars
☐ 1 pound pasta, your choice

☐ **WEEK COMPLETED**

Date:_____

WEEK 37
SITE SECURITY SURVEY

All the preps in the world won't help you if someone can easily take them from you. It's important to implement at least basic security measures for your home and retreat.

The first step is to determine your vulnerabilities and weaknesses. Once you have those figured out, you can work toward plugging those holes, so to speak.

This week, we're going to focus on structure hardening. This term refers to the security of your home's physical structure. You'll first do a survey of your home, and next week you'll work on fixing any problems you found.

Grab a notepad and pen and take a walk around your house. Make a note of every single point of entry, including all doors and ground-level windows. Don't forget basement windows.

- ☐ Are there bushes in front of any of those windows that might provide concealment for someone looking to break in?
- ☐ Do you have exterior lighting at all doors? Do the lights work?
- ☐ Do you have keys hidden outside somewhere? How hidden are they really? Please don't tell me you have a key under the doormat or in one of those fake rocks!
- ☐ Do you have trees with branches that overhang your roof that can allow someone access to the upper levels?

- ❏ Do you have window air conditioners? Can they be easily removed from the outside?
- ❏ Do you have solid-core or metal-encased exterior doors? Do the doors have windows built in?
- ❏ Do you have dead bolts on all exterior doors?
- ❏ Are the hinges on exterior doors exposed to the outside?
- ❏ Are all windows lockable from the inside? What kinds of windows do you have (casement, sliding, etc.)?
- ❏ Do you routinely keep curtains/drapes over windows so people can't see inside?
- ❏ If you live in an apartment or condo, are the hallways well lit?
- ❏ Is it a secured building? That is, is the building's outer door locked at all times, requiring a key or buzzer for entry?
- ❏ Do you have a pretty good idea of who lives around you? Would you recognize someone different in the immediate area?
- ❏ Is the parking area well lit, or are there deep shadows at night in spots?
- ❏ Does everyone in your family know what to do in case of fire? How about a break-in?

As you go through the survey, look at everything with an outsider's perspective. What would strangers see when they look at your home?

WEEK 37 ASSIGNMENTS

TASKS

☐ Go through the security survey above. Feel free to make notes of additional concerns I may not have mentioned. In the next lesson, we'll talk about ways to fix problem areas.

☐ Be sure you're rotating through your food supplies. Take some time this week to go through the pantry and identify anything that's approaching its best-by date. Plan to use it before it goes bad.

SAVINGS

☐ Add $10 to your Prepper Savings Account.

Total Prepper Savings Account: ☐

WATER STORAGE

☐ Store 1 gallon (or two 2-liter bottles) of water per person or a case of bottled water for the household.

Total Water Storage: ☐

GROCERY LIST

☐ 3 cans vegetables, your choice
☐ 2 cans fruit, your choice, but stick with those packed in water or juice, rather than syrup
☐ 1 can chili or stew, your choice
☐ 1 package or jar gravy, your choice
☐ 1 box tea bags (even if you don't drink tea, this is an excellent barter item)
☐ 1 jar pasta sauce, your choice
☐ 1 canister flavored drink mix, the type that has sugar already added
☐ 1 pound white rice

☐ **WEEK COMPLETED**
Date:_____

WEEK 38
STRUCTURE HARDENING PART I: DOORS AND WINDOWS

When I say structure hardening, I mean putting in place security measures to prevent break-ins. While no structure can be made impregnable without the use of some very high-tech and expensive gear and supplies, the average home owner can do many things to improve home security greatly.

Here, we will concentrate on the most common ways to enter a dwelling, the doors and windows.

DOORS

All exterior doors should be solid wood or steel encased. Doors that have large windows in them should be replaced if at all possible.

If the hinges on the exterior door are accessible from the outside, the hinge pins should be welded or glued in place. Hinges should be attached to the frame using screws long enough to go through the frame and into the stud.

The strength of a door comes from not only the material it's made of but also the number of points of attachment there are to the frame. These points of attachment include hinges as well as the doorknob and dead bolts. The more points of attachment, the stronger the door. At a minimum, make sure you have a dead bolt near the doorknob and ensure that the bolt goes into the frame at least a full inch.

If need be, during or after a disaster, you can fortify the door from the inside to prevent it from being kicked in. Purchase metal brackets and install them on either side of the door, making sure you're screwing the brackets into the studs rather than into drywall. Lay a two-by-four or two-by-six in the brackets so it goes across the door. The effect is not unlike what you've seen in countless westerns where the heroes place a large plank across the inside of the fort gate. You need not install these brackets until they're needed, just have them, the board, and the screws stashed in a front closet in case they're needed.

WINDOWS

Windows are problematic. Glass is easily broken, of course. There are materials available, though, such as Lexan, that can replace the glass and are virtually unbreakable. Although pricey, Kevlar-type materials can also be added to glass panes for the same effect. Another option is to place shatter-resistant film over the glass. You can find this type of product from a number of retailers. Simply do an online search for "shatter-resistant film."

Consider purchasing plywood to place over the inside of the windows and screw in place. Obviously, this will prevent you from seeing out, but it'll be difficult for someone to easily break through and gain entry. Cut the plywood to size, label each piece with which window it's for, and then stash them in the garage until they may be needed. Again, as with the doors, make sure all screws go into studs for strength. Of course, this is a measure you'd take after a disaster, as it isn't suited for everyday life.

A wide variety of shutters are available for most types of windows. They're designed to be used during hurricanes but will work well for our purposes, too. Of course, there are different configurations of bars you can install as well, but many home owners avoid them because of their unsightly appearance.

Double-hung windows can be secured by drilling a hole in the window frame, then sliding a nail that's slightly thinner into the hole. The nail prevents the window from sliding open, but you can remove the nail to open the window for ventilation when you're home.

Sliding windows, which move from left to right rather than up and down, can be secured by placing a dowel in the track of the sliding pane. This same tactic can be used on patio doors.

Casement windows are the ones that crank open by turning a handle. When closed, they're almost impossible to open from the outside. Left open, though, the metal arms are accessible from the outside and could be removed.

Hanging curtains over the windows when you're not home and at night will help keep prying eyes from seeing what you have inside. In the wake of a disaster, to prevent light from escaping at night and thus advertising your presence in the home, consider tacking up a couple of layers of landscape fabric over the windows.

OUTBUILDINGS

Don't forget to install security measures on outbuildings as well as the main dwelling. If a burglar or other ne'er-do-wells didn't bring a crowbar or sledgehammer, you don't want them picking one up in your shed to use. Keep doors and windows in outbuildings locked when you're not using them.

WEEK 38 ASSIGNMENTS

TASKS

☐ Determine which of the above options could be applied to your individual situation and begin implementing them. Purchase the necessary supplies and ask for installation assistance if need be.

☐ Continue working your way through the site security survey we discussed last week. Pay particular attention to how people approach your home (driveway, front walk, etc.) and what they can see as they do so.

SAVINGS

☐ Add $15 to your Prepper Savings Account.

Total Prepper Savings Account: ⬜

WATER STORAGE

☐ Store 1 gallon (or two 2-liter bottles) of water per person or a case of bottled water for the household.

Total Water Storage: ⬜

GROCERY LIST

☐ 3 cans vegetables, your choice

☐ 2 cans fruit, your choice, but stick with those packed in water or juice, rather than syrup

☐ 2 cans meat (tuna, chicken, beef), your choice

☐ 2 cans soup, not condensed (they require water)

☐ 1 box crackers, your choice

☐ 1 box (12 packages) ramen noodles

☐ 1 pound dry beans, your choice

☐ **WEEK COMPLETED**

Date:_____

WEEK 39
STRUCTURE HARDENING PART II: ALARMS

In large part, we implement security measures not just to prevent unauthorized access to our dwellings but also to at least slow intruders down long enough for us to become aware of them and take action. As I stated in last week's lesson, it's almost impossible to make the average house 100 percent impregnable. This week, we discuss what you can put in place to alert you to someone who's up to no good.

I'm a big fan of dogs, both as family pets and for security. You need not, and probably should not, go out and get the largest, meanest dog you can find. A Chihuahua will do just as well as a German shepherd when it comes to alerting you that something's amiss. Scientifically speaking, a dog's sense of smell is about a bazillion times stronger than ours, and their hearing is much sharper as well. They're capable of detecting danger much more effectively than we can.

With that said, though, my take on dogs is such that my mutts are part of my family. They're not employees, nor are they cattle. They are to be treated with love and affection, and, in return, they are wholeheartedly devoted to me and my family. Bringing a dog into your home is a lifetime commitment that should not be entered into lightly. If you take the time to bond with your dog and train it properly, it'll return the favor by being a vigilant protector.

Many studies show that a dog's presence is the number one factor to discourage a burglar from attempting to enter a home, influencing them instead to move on to another target.

Remotely monitored alarm systems can be worth the investment, but they're costly and contingent on electricity to operate. And, by their very nature, they require the involvement of another person to both monitor the system and alert you if something happens. I'm not ready to invest that amount of trust in someone I've never met.

There are relatively inexpensive alarms you can purchase. They run on batteries, so their effectiveness isn't tied to the grid.

In addition, you can install any number of Wi-Fi enabled cameras, both inside and outside. Many of them are motion sensitive and will alert you to movement so you can watch and see what's happening. But they're dependent upon the grid being up and running. If you don't have power or Wi-Fi, then those cameras aren't going to work.

You can go even cheaper, though, and use a DIY approach. Take a few empty aluminum soda cans and put some pebbles inside them. You don't need to use a ton of pebbles, just a few will work. Place these empty cans on windowsills so if intruders are able to gain access, they'll knock over the cans and make a loud racket. Depending on your window's configuration, you might even be able to balance a can just so, which will cause it to fall to the floor if someone so much as jiggles the window.

You can do something similar for doors by placing the can or a glass bottle a few inches behind the door when you retire for the evening. In the morning, place the can or bottle up against the wall behind the door so it's out of the way.

If you have the means to do so, consider putting in a gravel or crushed-shell walkway in front of your home. You might be surprised at how loud the noise is from someone walking on it, especially on a quiet night.

For as long as the grid is up, motion lights mounted above every exterior door work great. There are solar-powered lights as well, but many of them aren't very powerful. If you can, position the motion sensor so it detects anyone going near windows as well.

WEEK 39 ASSIGNMENTS

TASKS

☐ Work on obtaining what you need to install alarms for exterior doors and ground-level windows. Everyone's situation is unique, so use the information above as a guideline but tailor your solutions to your specific situation.

☐ If you have one or more dogs, work on their training this week and going forward. You want them to alert you to possible danger but also be quiet on command.

SAVINGS

☐ Add $10 to your Prepper Savings Account.

Total Prepper Savings Account: [_____]

WATER STORAGE

☐ Store 1 gallon (or two 2-liter bottles) of water per person or a case of bottled water for the household.

Total Water Storage: [_____]

GROCERY LIST

- ☐ 3 cans vegetables, your choice
- ☐ 2 cans fruit, your choice, but stick with those packed in water or juice, rather than syrup
- ☐ 1 can chili or stew, your choice
- ☐ 1 package or jar gravy, your choice
- ☐ 1 box powdered milk
- ☐ 1 pound pasta, your choice

☐ **WEEK COMPLETED**

Date:_____

WEEK 40
REDUCING YOUR FOOTPRINT

One aspect of prepper security after a major collapse is keeping your head down and blending in. For example, if it's been a few weeks since disaster struck and everyone around you is starting to see their belly buttons getting closer to their spines, you don't want to walk around picking bacon from between your teeth and patting a full stomach.

If folks around you have a strong feeling that you have more stuff than they do, it may be only a matter of time before they come knocking on your door, either with their hands out or their hands filled with weapons. By reducing your footprint, you reduce any motivation for folks to come visiting.

What do I mean by reducing your footprint? In this case, it means leaving little evidence lying around that indicates you're better off than others.

For at least the short term, bag up food wrappers and empty boxes for later disposal. If it looks like it'll be some time before trash pickup begins again, consider either burning or burying trash. Compost as much as you can.

If at all possible, in the wake of a major event do all cooking indoors to prevent the smell from wafting over the neighborhood. Depending on what you're cooking, which spices you use, and how you're cooking it, that odor can travel far. If you have to cook outside, do so as quickly as possible.

Try to keep things audibly quiet as well. Depending on the circumstances, it may be fine to let the kids play in the backyard, but make sure they understand to keep the noise down. Ne'er-do-wells hunting for targets might figure if your kids have enough energy to play a loud game of tag, they're getting that energy from food you're hiding.

Keep your stored food and water out of sight in the home. Folks looking through windows as they pass by shouldn't see five cases of MREs sitting on the kitchen table. And there may be occasions when neighbors might be welcome to stop over for a short visit, but you don't want them knowing that you have a dozen cases of bottled water socked away.

If your neighbors are not keeping up with their lawns and flower beds, don't be the only one on the block who does. Keep gardens in the backyard or somewhere else that's not easily seen from the street. Consider privacy fencing to keep eyes away from your stuff.

Again, a key element here is to blend in with those around you. If they're wearing drab clothes that are starting to get ragged, that's not the best time to strut around in new-looking cargo pants and flannel shirts you set aside for a rainy day.

Personally, I have a hard time with preppers who line up for any rations being given out by authorities if said preppers have a fully stocked pantry. Doing so reduces the available resources for the truly needy. But I fully understand the desire to blend in with the crowd and not be the only ones conspicuously absent from the soup line. You'll have to make your own call on that one. Perhaps you can save the handouts to discreetly give to others.

WEEK 40 ASSIGNMENTS

TASKS

☐ Work on reducing your footprint now to get in practice. Do what you can to generate less waste, for example. By way of comparison, my own family of five fills one, maybe two, trash bags a week with normal garbage. Add to that one recyclable bin, and that's about all we put out for collection each week. Much of that trash could be burned if we had to do so.

☐ Give some hard thought to repurposing items you'd normally put in the trash. Brainstorm with family members about how you can reuse tin cans and other containers, for example.

SAVINGS

☐ Add $15 to your Prepper Savings Account.

Total Prepper Savings Account: ☐

WATER STORAGE

☐ Store 1 gallon (or two 2-liter bottles) of water per person or a case of bottled water for the household.

Total Water Storage: ☐

GROCERY LIST

- ☐ 3 cans vegetables, your choice
- ☐ 2 cans fruit, your choice, but stick with those packed in water or juice, rather than syrup
- ☐ 2 cans meat (tuna, chicken, beef), your choice
- ☐ 2 cans soup, not condensed (they require water)
- ☐ 1 package dry soup mix, your choice
- ☐ 1 gallon cooking oil (vegetable oil is preferred, for longer shelf life)
- ☐ 1 pound white rice

☐ **WEEK COMPLETED**

Date:_____

WEEK 41
PRACTICING SITUATIONAL AWARENESS

How observant are you in your day-to-day life? Many people, and preppers are no exception, walk around with blinders on and pay little attention to the world around them. This is something you'll need to change about yourself if that's the case with you.

In what seems like a lifetime ago, I spent about a decade working in retail security. I spent countless hours being paid fairly well to watch people, both on camera and from the sales floor. Because of this experience, I became adept at reading people and even anticipating their movements and actions. I also learned just how little attention people paid to what went on around them. Countless times I saw a shoplifter conceal merchandise in his or her coat or pocket within a few feet of other shoppers. These other people had absolutely no clue what was happening nearby while they were looking at the merchandise in front of them.

Part of situational awareness involves what we call establishing baselines. The term baseline refers to what you would consider the norm in a given environment or situation. Deviations from the baseline should get our attention when our situational awareness is on track. Probably most often, these are visual cues, such as a door that's ajar when it should be firmly closed. But they could also be olfactory indicators, such as the smell of smoke, or auditory, like hearing footsteps when you thought you were alone. The point here is that you should pay attention to these baseline deviations, as they could indicate problems.

Colonel Jeff Cooper, one of the most well-respected firearms instructors our country has ever seen, developed what is known as the Cooper Color Code. It's a way to refer to the level of awareness you have at any point in your daily life.

Condition White: You're paying very little attention to the world around you. You're relaxed and calm with little or no worries.

Condition Yellow: You're aware of your surroundings, but there's nothing going on of real significance. You're alert to potential threats, but nothing concrete is on your radar.

Condition Orange: You're alert to a specific potential threat, but thus far there's no real danger. You're still scanning for other threats, but there's at least one that has caught your attention.

Condition Red: There's a real, immediate threat, and you're prepared to act against it. You may not have to physically react, yet you're ready to do so if need be.

Here's how these conditions could unfold in the real world. You and your spouse are sitting at home one evening. It's around 9:00 p.m., and the two of you are deeply involved in the last act of a movie you found on Netflix. You're currently at Condition White.

Then there's a knock at the front door. You immediately shift to Condition Yellow. There's no real threat at the moment, but you weren't expecting any visitors, especially late at night, so it is definitely a deviation from the baseline.

You look out the window and see an adult male standing on the front porch. You've never seen him before, and he certainly doesn't look like he's there to ask whether you've been "saved" or not. You move into Condition Orange. You don't know who he is, but he hasn't made any overt threats. Could be he needs help, maybe his car broke down.

While standing away from the door, you call to him and ask what he wants. He tells you he's there to read the water meter, an obvious lie.

You're now at Condition Red and take whatever action you feel is necessary. If, on the other hand, he does say his car broke down, and he's hoping to either borrow your phone or ask you to call a tow for him, then you'd stay at Condition Orange until he's left the area.

Make sense?

It wouldn't be the worst idea in the world to get into the habit of telling yourself, nonverbally of course, when you move from one color to another. Doing so will help keep your mind focused.

Situational awareness is a key element of an overall safety and security plan. You absolutely cannot predict when trouble may visit you or your loved ones. It's only through being vigilant and observing the world as you travel through it that you'll be in a position to act quickly and decisively when it becomes necessary for you to do so.

It does take practice. Awareness is not a skill you'll develop overnight. Here are some practice exercises:

- When you and your family are driving somewhere, make a mental note of the vehicles passing you in the opposite direction. Color, condition, that sort of thing. Quiz each other from time to time with questions like, "What color was the last vehicle that passed us?" Looking in the rearview mirror is cheating.
- When on foot, make it a habit to "check your six" regularly. Checking your six is taking a look at whoever is behind you. At a mall or another similar location, this is easily done by stopping to look in a shop window, then glancing behind you before you move on. Pay attention to anyone who seems to stop over and over when you do.
- When you're out shopping, make a point to notice who's in the same aisle as you. Male or female, alone or with kids, attire, demeanor. Then quiz yourself or each other when you get a few aisles away. What color was his shirt? Was she with a boy and a girl or two boys?

The takeaway from this week's lesson is to rip off the blinders and pay attention to what's going on around you as much as possible.

WEEK 41 ASSIGNMENTS

TASKS

☐ Practice the situational awareness exercises and develop a few more of your own. Kids can really get into this if you present it as a game.

☐ If you're active on any social media websites, such as Facebook, take a hard look at your profile information. What are you telling the world about you? Be very aware of what people can find out about you by simply clicking a mouse.

SAVINGS

☐ Add $10 to your Prepper Savings Account.

Total Prepper Savings Account: _____

WATER STORAGE

☐ Store 1 gallon (or two 2-liter bottles) of water per person or a case of bottled water for the household.

Total Water Storage: _____

GROCERY LIST

- ☐ 3 cans vegetables, your choice
- ☐ 2 cans fruit, your choice, but stick with those packed in water or juice, rather than syrup
- ☐ 1 can chili or stew, your choice
- ☐ 1 package or jar gravy, your choice
- ☐ 1 box granola bars, protein bars, or equivalent
- ☐ 1 pound dry beans, your choice

☐ **WEEK COMPLETED**

Date:_____

SECTION V
WINTER

WEEK 42
PLANNING FOR POSTCOLLAPSE EXCURSIONS

During any lingering sort of disaster, such as a lengthy pandemic or perhaps an electromagnetic pulse (EMP) strike, there may come times when members of the family or group will need to venture out into the world. For example, perhaps supplies of certain medications are running low. Or it could just be the need to gather information about the world at large.

The prudent prepper needs to foresee this possibility and plan for it. For our discussion here, I call those who go exploring "scouts."

It's important that any excursion be planned out in great detail. The ideal scouts will be those who are quick and intelligent and know the area well. They need to be able to think on their feet, making snap decisions as necessary.

Maps of the area are essential for planning. Take the time now to acquire as many detailed maps as you can find, including road atlases and street maps. It would also behoove you to take those maps with you when you're out and about now, jotting notes about the area. Knowing where you can potentially find supplies if things go from bad to worse will be helpful.

Another thing to consider, when the time comes, is to combine the existing maps with any information you gather or glean from various sources and draw up new maps, complete with notations on who's now residing where, known deaths in the area, and other vital information. As scouts return, they can add their observations to the maps, keeping things as current as possible.

When a scouting mission is being planned, the scouts should be given lists of needed items as well as a way to bring those items back. This is when having a stash of empty backpacks may come in handy. When possible, scouts should also have communications equipment so they can stay in touch not only with home but with each other. Two-way radios or portable CB radios may work well for this, depending on the range involved.

Using the information available, specific routes should be planned and memorized, with alternates included. It's important that the scouts stick to the plan as much as possible. In the event that things go awry, the remaining family members will want and need to have at least some idea of where to search.

With rare exception, the scouts should strive to remain unseen, or at least unnoticed. This means they should try to blend in, mirroring the appearance of those around them. Disheveled and dirty will likely be the name of the game. This also extends to being aware of noise that may be generated by the scouts' searching. They should avoid kicking in doors or smashing windows, for example.

Time is of the essence. Scouts need to get in, grab what's needed, and get back home as quickly as is prudent. Every moment spent outside the home or retreat increases the risk of detection. The route back to the retreat, though, should not be a direct one, in case the scouts are detected or followed. Taking a more circuitous route will help in determining if they're being tracked.

It's a good idea to develop some sort of code that the scouts can use with those at home upon their arrival that would indicate either all is well or they're under duress. This could be as simple as placing a colored bandanna in the front pocket to show that the scouts are fine, while no bandanna would indicate something is amiss. A corresponding code from the group or retreat would not be a bad idea either.

If numbers allow, two or more scouts in a group would be ideal. They can then back each other up as well as keep additional eyes out for danger. With that in mind, planning should include contingencies in the event that the scouts are separated. A few different meeting points should be chosen on the map and communicated to each scout. If separated, scouts should immediately proceed to the nearest meeting point and wait for a given period of time to see if everyone is able to make it. If someone doesn't show up within that time, the remaining scouts should proceed back to the retreat to regroup and plan the next move.

WEEK 42 ASSIGNMENTS

TASKS

☐ Obtain several maps of your local area, the more detailed the better. Begin planning routes on foot to locations that you feel are most likely for you to have to visit after a collapse.

☐ Think about the people you'll have in your group and decide who you feel would make for the best scouts. Give thought to how they should be equipped for a mission.

SAVINGS

☐ Add $10 to your Prepper Savings Account.

Total Prepper Savings Account: ☐

WATER STORAGE

☐ Store 1 gallon (or two 2-liter bottles) of water per person or a case of bottled water for the household.

Total Water Storage: ☐

GROCERY LIST

☐ 3 cans vegetables, your choice

☐ 2 cans fruit, your choice, but stick with those packed in water or juice, rather than syrup

☐ 2 cans meat (tuna, chicken, beef), your choice

☐ 2 cans soup, not condensed (they require water)

☐ 1 canister oatmeal or 1 box flavored instant oatmeal

☐ 1 jar pasta sauce, your choice

☐ 1 canister table salt

☐ 1 pound pasta, your choice

☐ **WEEK COMPLETED**

Date:_____

WEEK 43

ODDS AND ENDS TO STOCK UP ON

You'll want to have several things on hand in large quantities during and after a disaster. Many of these don't neatly fit into specific categories, so I'm lumping them together in today's lesson.

Sewing materials: These are things like needles, thread, and patches. Depending on the nature of the disaster, it might be some time before you'll be able to buy new clothes. Get the necessary supplies and learn the skills for repairing clothing now. Remember, too, that you might not have the luxury of an electric sewing machine.

Duct tape: Duct tape has so many uses; make sure you have several rolls.

Tarps: These are very good to have in the event of storm damage to the home. Get the larger sizes—it's easy enough to fold them into smaller sizes, but it's impossible to make small ones larger.

Bungee cords: Use these with the tarps.

Plywood and dimensional lumber: If tarps won't quite do the trick, plywood and two-by-fours usually will when it comes to temporary repairs for storm damage. Don't forget nails, screws, and tools.

Paracord: Vastly superior to clothesline, paracord is very strong yet small in size. You can use it for everything from replacement shoelaces to lashing items to the car during an evacuation.

Manual can openers: A pantry filled floor to ceiling with canned goods won't help you much if you can't open the cans. Have several manual can openers set aside in case of loss or breakage.

Trash bags: These have several uses, including lining the toilet when the plumbing isn't working, bagging up trash, and serving as temporary rain ponchos. If possible, pay a little extra to get contractor grade—the plastic is much more durable in them than in typical kitchen garbage bags.

Coolers: In the event of a power outage, having a few coolers will help you preserve at least some of your food before it goes bad. Picking them up at rummage sales will save you a few bucks.

WEEK 43 ASSIGNMENTS

TASKS

☐ Begin stockpiling as many items from the above list as possible. If you think you have enough, get a few more of each just to be safe. Better to have it and not need it than need it and not have it.

☐ Revisit the inventory lists you made at the beginning of this book. Update them as needed and work on filling in any gaps you see.

SAVINGS

☐ Add $15 to your Prepper Savings Account.

Total Prepper Savings Account: _____

WATER STORAGE

☐ Store 1 gallon (or two 2-liter bottles) of water per person or a case of bottled water for the household.

Total Water Storage: _____

GROCERY LIST

☐ 3 cans vegetables, your choice.

☐ 2 cans fruit, your choice, but stick with those packed in water or juice, rather than syrup

☐ 1 can chili or stew, your choice

☐ 1 package or jar gravy, your choice

☐ 1 jar peanut butter (if allergies are an issue, substitute an allergen-free version, such as sunflower butter)

☐ 1 box (12 packages) ramen noodles

☐ 1 jar honey (100 percent real honey, not flavored corn syrup)

☐ 1 pound white rice

☐ **WEEK COMPLETED**

Date:_____

WEEK 44

VEHICLE EMERGENCY KITS

We spend a heck of a lot of time in our cars, trucks, and vans, don't we? From commuting back and forth to work to playing chauffeur for our kids, it seems like we're perpetually watching the world go by as we flit around from one destination to another. With all this time spent on the road, the odds are good that at some point or another, you're going to have a breakdown or end up stranded for some reason. Could be the weather is so bad, you're safer just finding a place to pull over until things clear up.

A vehicle emergency kit differs from an actual survival kit in both purpose and design. A survival kit is there to provide for your basic needs until you reach a safe place, while the vehicle emergency kit is there to give you the tools to get back on the road or keep you safe until help arrives.

Even if you don't know much more about vehicles than how to put gas in the tank, it's wise to have a collection of basic tools with you. If you're stranded on the side of the road, someone may come along who has the knowledge and skills to make a necessary repair but lacks the tools for doing so. Don't hamper a Good Samaritan by not having at least the basics with you.

Start with a small toolbox or bag. Don't go out and buy a snazzy new metal Craftsman toolbox, either. You're not carting this in and out of a work site daily. It's going to sit in your trunk until needed. The toolbox should contain these items:

- ☐ Set of wrenches, both SAE and metric (while you could just go with a couple of adjustable wrenches, they sometimes have a tendency to slip off the nut or bolt, which can make things frustrating for all involved)
- ☐ Different sizes of pliers, from channel locks to needle-nose
- ☐ Several screwdrivers, both slotted and Phillips, of varying sizes
- ☐ Roll of duct tape
- ☐ Roll of electrical tape
- ☐ Sharp knife
- ☐ Flashlight with extra batteries
- ☐ Hammer
- ☐ Small can of WD-40 or other lubricant
- ☐ Small pipe with an inner diameter large enough to accommodate wrenches (a great tool for when you need extra leverage on a stubborn nut or bolt)
- ☐ Several plastic zip ties
- ☐ Wire coat hanger or two (I'm old-fashioned, and these still work great in case of muffler detachment)
- ☐ Jumper cables

Any time you're working with tools or machinery, some sort of safety gear should be involved. If you've ever worked under a car and had rust fall into your eyes, you know all too well just how ... interesting ... that pain can be. Gasoline sprayed into your face when you're changing a fuel filter is another fun experience. Be sure to add to your kit a pair or two of safety glasses or goggles, as well as a few pairs of work gloves.

While it's not feasible to carry around an entire auto parts store in your trunk, a few key items will help with the most common vehicle problems:

- ☐ 2–3 quarts motor oil
- ☐ Jug of antifreeze, premixed with water
- ☐ Fix-a-Flat
- ☐ Spare fuses
- ☐ Vehicle repair book for your car, truck, or van

If you've never looked before, you might want to verify that you have not only a spare tire but also a jack. Many cars sold today, used or new, seem to be lacking these basic items.

Your vehicle emergency kit should also contain a few things that you can use to signal for help. A brightly colored bandanna can be tied to the vehicle's antenna or outside mirror to help folks find you more easily. In some circumstances, the vehicle's horn may be inoperable, and a decent whistle will be far louder than the sound of your voice.

Finally, should you end up stuck in your vehicle for hours waiting for help to arrive, a blanket and a few distractions will help the time go by. A book, crossword puzzles, and the like can take the sting out of being stranded.

WEEK 44 ASSIGNMENTS

TASKS

☐ Put together an emergency kit for each of your vehicles. Be sure each driver knows where the kit is located, what's in it, and how to use things like jumper cables and Fix-a-Flat.

☐ If you're physically able, look into having someone teach you and the other drivers in your family how to perform basic repairs on your vehicles, such as changing a tire, replacing a battery, and installing a new belt. These skills may prove extremely useful at some point.

SAVINGS

☐ Add $10 to your Prepper Savings Account.

Total Prepper Savings Account: [   ]

WATER STORAGE

☐ Store 1 gallon (or two 2-liter bottles) of water per person or a case of bottled water for the household.

Total Water Storage: [   ]

GROCERY LIST

☐ 3 cans vegetables, your choice
☐ 2 cans fruit, your choice, but stick with those packed in water or juice, rather than syrup
☐ 2 cans meat (tuna, chicken, beef), your choice
☐ 2 cans soup, not condensed (they require water)
☐ 1 jar jelly or fruit preserves
☐ 1 package dry soup mix, your choice
☐ 1 sack cornmeal
☐ 1 pound dry beans, your choice

☐ **WEEK COMPLETED**

Date:_____

WEEK 45
THE DEATH FILE

You can call yours whatever you like. I know the Death File sounds a little morbid. What this project amounts to is a carefully curated collection of information your family will need upon your passing. This isn't necessarily a fun process, but it needs to be done.

My dad died in 2019. His health had been pretty bad for several months, so it wasn't a shock. In the year or two before he died, I tried bringing up his last wishes and such several times, and he wanted nothing to do with that conversation. He told me where to find his will and insisted everything I needed would be there.

Yeah, not so much. All that was in the file was a very sparse, two-page will. That's it. My wife and I spent the better part of a year trying to get his affairs sorted out, with varied results. Every week there was something new that needed to be addressed, such as an account that needed to be closed or another repair to his house that needed attention before we could list it for sale. Dealing with all this left very little time and energy to actually grieve for our loss.

Don't do that to your family. Set up a Death File so they know what to do and how to do it. The Death File should contain a few essential items.

Legal documents: These include a will, power of attorney, living will, and any other health care directives. Don't forget any special instructions for your last wishes, such as scattering some of your cremated ashes in a special place.

Insurance policies: Make a list of every single insurance policy you have. Include the policy number and the relevant information for filing claims. If your family doesn't know an insurance policy exists, they can't file a claim.

Bank accounts: Make a list of every bank account in your name, including checking, savings, investment, and retirement. You don't necessarily need to include balance information, but you should note the bank name and the account number, at a minimum. Talk to someone at your banks now about how best to arrange account access for your estate executor when you pass.

Safes: If you have any safes, your family will need to know how to get into them. My dad had two safes, and I ended up having to contact the manufacturer of one of them to get the combination. This took a few weeks to accomplish.

Bills: Put together a list of every single account in your name where you make payments. This includes mortgage, loans, credit cards, utilities, even gym memberships. Many of us set these bills up to auto-pay from our accounts. But if you're gone, there's no need for anyone to pay your gym membership, right?

Real estate: If you own your home, talk to an attorney about a transfer-on-death deed. This isn't available in all fifty states, but it can be a valuable tool if it is available to you. In a very basic sense, what it does is automatically transfer ownership of your home and property to the person you've elected to receive it, bypassing probate. This can save thousands of dollars.

Online accounts: Include log in information for all your online accounts, such as social media and email. This allows your family members to access and respond to messages, as well as make posts on your behalf. Same goes with unlocking your cell phone.

Contacts: Make a list of every person you feel should be notified of your passing, as well as how to get in touch with them. While close family members probably know who many of your real-life friends are, online contacts can be another matter entirely. Don't forget about employers and coworkers.

Last words: This is something that many never think to do, but it could be so important. Consider writing a note to your loved ones to let them know how much you care about them, how proud you are of them, that sort of thing. If you often have trouble expressing yourself in this manner when you're face-to-face, this is a great way to tell them you love them. Not only will they treasure such a message, but it will help them to find closure in your passing.

Make sure your family knows where to find your Death File. A fire-resistant safe is probably a good idea. Don't forget to tell them where to find the key.

WEEK 45 ASSIGNMENTS

TASKS

☐ Start assembling your Death File. This is a big project, so don't expect to finish it in a day or two. But don't put it off any longer than absolutely necessary.

☐ If you haven't done so already, put together a will. If you can't afford to hire an attorney to do this, seek out simple forms online or at the public library to get you started.

SAVINGS

☐ Add $15 to your Prepper Savings Account.

Total Prepper Savings Account: ☐

WATER STORAGE

☐ Store 1 gallon (or two 2-liter bottles) of water per person or a case of bottled water for the household.

Total Water Storage: ☐

GROCERY LIST

☐ 3 cans vegetables, your choice
☐ 2 cans fruit, your choice, but stick with those packed in water or juice, rather than syrup
☐ 1 can chili or stew, your choice
☐ 1 package or jar gravy, your choice
☐ 1 box baking mix, preferably the type that doesn't require eggs, milk, or other ingredients
☐ 1 box granola bars, protein bars, or equivalent
☐ 1 gallon cooking oil (vegetable oil is preferred, for longer shelf life)
☐ 1 pound pasta, your choice

☐ **WEEK COMPLETED**

Date:_____

WEEK 46
BUILDING MICROCLIMATES

Cold weather can kill, make no mistake about it. Therefore, it's critical that you know how to keep warm. What it often boils down to is creating what is called a microclimate. That's a fancy way of saying you need to close off a small area that you can then heat through some means, raising the temperature enough to keep you alive. The smaller the area, and the better insulated it is, the easier it'll be to keep it warm.

If your furnace goes out or there's a lengthy power outage, your home can cool off pretty quickly, going from uncomfortable to outright dangerous in a matter of hours in some cases. Fortunately, building an indoor microclimate is pretty easy.

The basic approach is to pile everyone into the smallest bedroom. Close the door and cover it with a blanket. Do the same to the windows. This helps to insulate against drafts. Depending on the size of the room and the number of people you have in it, body heat alone will start to raise the temperature in short order. It should go without saying that bundling up and cuddling under blankets is definitely advisable. Don't forget to bring into the room your dogs, cats, and other indoor critters.

Another approach is to set up a tent in the living room. Cover it with a blanket or comforter to insulate it a little better, then toss blankets and pillows inside for everyone to use. A vicious cold snap hit Texas a few years ago, and several families used this idea to stay warm. If you don't have a tent, cobble together a fort with couch cushions and pillows. Your kids will tell the story about the night the entire family slept in a pillow fort for the rest of their lives.

If you find yourself lost in the woods, or for any other reason you're left to your own devices overnight in the field, the ability to cobble together a shelter may save your life. Weather conditions may make it almost impossible to get a fire going to keep you warm. Or there may be other reasons that you may not wish to advertise your presence with a campfire. Being able to get out of the elements not only will be a great boon to your state of mind but also will help prevent hypothermia and other ill effects.

One of the simplest shelters is called a debris hut. You'll need a long branch or log, at least a few feet longer than you are tall. It should be fairly thick and sturdy, to serve as the "spine" of your shelter. Prop one end of the branch or log on a large rock or against a branch of a standing tree. Ideally, the log will be about three feet or so off the ground. This end is going to be the opening of your shelter. If possible, arrange the shelter so this opening faces away from the prevailing winds.

Next, lean branches against the spine of your structure. Go along both sides, from the mouth of the shelter all the way to the other end. These are the "ribs" of your shelter. Keep the ribs as close together as you can. Now, pile leaves, moss, grass, even dirt, onto the ribs. This is the insulation, so lay it on thick. The more insulation, the warmer your shelter.

Finally, lay more sticks down on top of the insulation to keep it in place. If you don't have something to use for a ground cover, like an emergency blanket, pile grass and moss on the floor of your shelter.

Slide into the shelter feet first, and wiggle your way in. Go as far into the shelter as you can. While this isn't exactly five-star accommodations, it'll keep you warm and relatively dry until morning.

A variation on this is the simple lean-to. This was my favorite type of fort to build when I was a kid tramping through the woods near my home. My friends and I built many of them, using them as "Army bases" when we were playing commando. Take a thick branch about six or seven feet long and suspend it about four feet from the ground between two trees.

If there aren't branches creating convenient crooks to do so, you'll need to use cordage to lash this crossbeam to the uprights. Take long branches and lean them against this suspended branch. We found that the ideal for these branches was about eight or nine feet in length. Take shorter branches and lean them against the sides, to create more of a hut shape. Then pile on the insulating material. The lean-to can be quite comfortable, especially if you build a campfire near the opening and construct a reflecting wall of logs on the opposite side of the fire.

In the winter months, you can put together a snow cave. Simply make a large pile of snow, four or five feet high and six feet across. From the side of the pile that faces away from the wind, start digging a tunnel into the pile. All you need is a space big enough for you to curl up inside. Pile loose snow in front of the opening once you're inside. Again, it's not the most comfortable arrangement, but certainly better than the alternative.

When we were kids, we built forts like these using nothing but our hands. Sure, we might have had the use of a snow shovel for a snow cave, but that'd be about it. Having access to a sharp knife or hatchet as well as cordage like paracord would have made things much easier. And a couple of emergency blankets would also help a great deal.

The point of building a microclimate is to keep you warm for a night or two, not to live in long-term. Let's hope that a survival situation that requires the use of such shelters is over quickly.

WEEK 46 ASSIGNMENTS

TASKS

☐ Get outside and practice building temporary shelters. Get creative with the materials available to you. The smaller the interior size of the shelter, the less space you'll need to warm with your body heat. Make it just big enough to crawl into.

☐ Explore the area around your home and look for animal tracks. Get a book from your local library and practice identifying them. This'll give you a good idea of what's living in your area. There may come a time when you will need to augment your food supplies through hunting and trapping.

SAVINGS

☐ Add $15 to your Prepper Savings Account.

Total Prepper Savings Account: ☐

WATER STORAGE

☐ Store 1 gallon (or two 2-liter bottles) of water per person or a case of bottled water for the household.

Total Water Storage: ☐

GROCERY LIST

☐ 3 cans vegetables, your choice
☐ 2 cans fruit, your choice, but stick with those packed in water or juice, rather than syrup
☐ 2 cans meat (tuna, chicken, beef), your choice
☐ 2 cans soup, not condensed (they require water)
☐ 1 jar instant coffee (even if you don't drink coffee, this is an excellent barter item)
☐ 1 jar pasta sauce, your choice
☐ 1 canister flavored drink mix, the type that has sugar already added
☐ 1 pound white rice

☐ **WEEK COMPLETED**

Date:_____

WEEK 47
BULKING UP THE PANTRY

I've placed this lesson smack in the middle of the winter section for a reason. As we approach the holiday season, grocery stores will be running tremendous sales on many things that we'll want to stock up on for the pantry.

The first thing that comes to mind this time of year, of course, is turkey. Great big birds for pennies a pound. This is when having the means to can food at home is extremely handy. Pick up a couple of birds, then make and can batches of turkey meat, turkey soup, turkey à la king, that sort of stuff. Even a single 12-pound turkey can go a long way. Be sure to use the carcass to make soup stock, too. Don't let anything go to waste.

Next up are veggies. Canned vegetables will be cheap, so stock up. Granted, store-bought canned vegetables pale in comparison with home canned from the garden, but often they'll go on sale so cheap you can hardly pass them up.

Baking staples will be on sale as well in the coming weeks. Flour, sugar, baking powder, all that good stuff. I leave them in their original packaging and put them in five gallon buckets affixed with Gamma Seal lids for storage.

Before any "feast" holiday (Thanksgiving, Christmas, Easter, Memorial Day, Fourth of July, Labor Day), there's usually a decent sale on paper goods, too. Plates, cups, napkins, all that fun stuff. During a short-term emergency, you're not going to want to waste water on washing dishes. Stock up on plates and plastic utensils now.

After many of those holidays, you can pick up themed products on clearance, too. Candles can be had for a steal right after Christmas, for example.

One of the best ways the frugal prepper can stretch a dollar is by taking advantage of these seasonal sales.

WEEK 47 ASSIGNMENTS

TASKS

☐ Stock up on food and other goods as your budget and sales permit. Watch the sale ads and use coupons to get the best bang for your buck.

☐ If you haven't done so already, begin making out your gift lists for the holiday season. When and where possible, concentrate on prepping-related gifts, such as crank radios and emergency blankets.

SAVINGS

☐ Add $15 to your Prepper Savings Account.

Total Prepper Savings Account:

WATER STORAGE

☐ Store 1 gallon (or two 2-liter bottles) of water per person or a case of bottled water for the household.

Total Water Storage:

GROCERY LIST

☐ 3 cans vegetables, your choice
☐ 2 cans fruit, your choice, but stick with those packed in water or juice, rather than syrup
☐ 1 can chili or stew, your choice
☐ 1 package or jar gravy, your choice
☐ 1 box tea bags (even if you don't drink tea, this is an excellent barter item)
☐ 1 box (12 packages) ramen noodles
☐ 1 pound dry beans, your choice

☐ **WEEK COMPLETED**

Date:_____

WEEK 48
INVENTORY: THE BASICS

The absolute basics for survival consist of shelter, water, and food. Everything else is secondary. Note that I'm not including air on that list for the very simple reason that if you're in a situation where air is an issue, there isn't going to be a whole lot you can do about it other than get out of that area immediately.

If you don't have adequate shelter, you can die very quickly from exposure to the elements. While the typical concern is being able to keep warm and dry, overheating can be a serious issue as well. In the shelter category are fire-starting supplies, emergency blankets, tents, season-appropriate clothing—anything and everything that protects you from the weather.

The rule of thumb when it comes to water is that the body can survive about three days without hydration. While that may be technically true, the latter part of that time frame will be spent in agony. Never severely ration water. Drink what you can today and work on getting more before you need it. In the water column of our inventory we include not only stored water but the means to purify more.

While I'm sure most of us could stand to lose a few pounds, food is still a concern and one of our basic needs. We need calories to burn for fuel. Without fuel, our bodies and minds slow down and become sluggish. And decent food is always a morale boost.

This week, I want you to take a good, hard look at what you've prepped so far for shelter, water, and food.

If you lost power for a considerable length of time, how will you keep your family warm?

If you turned on your faucets and nothing came out, how long can you last on just the water you have stored?

If running to the grocery store is suddenly not an option, how long could you feed your family with what you have available in the house?

At an absolute minimum, you should strive to be able to meet your basic needs for at least one full month. Obviously, more is better.

If you're not there yet, then you need to ramp up your prepping to get to that goal as soon as possible.

As far as shelter needs, whatever the disaster, with luck you'll be able to shelter in place at home. You want to keep a roof over your head and some sort of walls around you. A fire will keep you warm as well as cook your food and provide light.

All in all, if you have adequate shelter, water, and food, you'll be ahead of the game, come what may.

WEEK 48 ASSIGNMENTS

TASKS

☐ Do a complete inventory of your food and water, as well as what you have in place for emergency shelter gear. If you fall short of a full month's worth of supplies, work hard and quickly to get to that goal.

☐ If you haven't done so recently, inspect and resupply your portable survival kits. Remember to add any necessary cold-weather gear.

SAVINGS

☐ Add $15 to your Prepper Savings Account.

Total Prepper Savings Account:

WATER STORAGE

☐ Store 1 gallon (or two 2-liter bottles) of water per person or a case of bottled water for the household.

Total Water Storage:

GROCERY LIST

☐ 3 cans vegetables, your choice
☐ 2 cans fruit, your choice, but stick with those packed in water or juice, rather than syrup
☐ 2 cans meat (tuna, chicken, beef), your choice
☐ 2 cans soup, not condensed (they require water)
☐ 1 box crackers, your choice
☐ 1 package dry soup mix, your choice
☐ 1 pound pasta, your choice

☐ **WEEK COMPLETED**

Date:_____

WEEK 49
THE SURVIVAL AND PREPAREDNESS LIBRARY

No matter how long we've been prepping, we can't know it all. Sure, common sense and a logical mind will go a long way toward filling in the gaps, but having reference materials is always a good idea.

When it comes to putting together a home library, there are many categories to be filled.

HOMESTEADING SKILLS

Animal husbandry, gardening/farming, butchering, things along those lines fall into this category. Suggestions include the following:
- *Backwoods Home Magazine* (BackwoodsHome.com)
- *The Encyclopedia of Country Living,* by Carla Emery, 50th anniversary ed. (Sasquatch Books, 2019)
- *Storey's Basic Country Skills: A Practical Guide to Self-Reliance* (Storey Publishing, 2010)
- *Mini Farming: Self Sufficiency on ¼ Acre,* by Brett Markham (Skyhorse Publishing, 2010)

FOOD STORAGE AND PRESERVATION

This could probably fall under homesteading skills, but it's important enough to warrant its own category. Canning, dehydrating, and other methods of preservation, as well as putting together and maintaining an effective food storage plan, are all vital skills. Here are some good resources:

- *Canning and Preserving for Dummies*, by Amelia Jeanroy and Karen Ward, 2nd ed. (For Dummies, 2009)
- *Root Cellaring: Natural Cold Storage of Fruits and Vegetables*, by Mike and Nancy Bubel, 2nd ed. (Storey Publishing, 1991)
- *Ball Complete Book of Home Preserving*, by Judi Kingery and Lauren Devine (Robert Rose, 2024)

FIREARMS MAINTENANCE

You should own complete manuals for every firearm you own, including detailed instructions on disassembling and cleaning. Just because *you* know how to do it doesn't necessarily mean everyone in your family or group does.

SECURITY AND DEFENSE

All the food, gear, and supplies in the world won't do you much good if someone else is able to take them away from you. In addition to home security, you should develop a good handle on situational awareness and understand the survival mindset. Recommendations include the following:

- *The Gift of Fear*, by Gavin de Becker (Dell, 1998)
- *Left of Bang*, by Patrick Van Horne and Jason Riley (Black Irish Entertainment, 2014)
- *Suburban Defense*, by Don Shift (independently published, 2021)
- *Becoming Bulletproof*, by Evy Poumpouras (Atria Books, 2024)
- *The Unthinkable*, by Amanda Ripley, 2nd ed. (Harmony, 2024)

WILD EDIBLES AND MEDICINALS

Ideally, these references will have color photographs for ease of identification as well as common uses and preparation instructions for each plant discussed. Here are some good resources:

- *Peterson Field Guide to Medicinal Plants & Herbs of Eastern & Central N. America,* by Steven Foster and James A. Duke, 3rd ed. (Mariner Books, 2014)
- *Peterson Field Guide to Western Medicinal Plants and Herbs,* by Christopher Hobbs and Steven Foster (Mariner Books, 2002)
- *Foraging Wild Edible Plants of North America,* by Christopher Nyerges, 2nd ed. (Falcon Guides, 2023)
- *The Forager's Harvest,* by Samuel Thayer (Foragers Harvest Press, 2006)

MEDICAL

These references cover everything from basic first aid to complex injuries and illnesses. Hospitals and doctors may turn out to be luxuries of days gone by. Don't forget information on herbal remedies and other homeopathic approaches. I highly recommend these:

- *Prepper's Natural Medicine,* by Cat Ellis (Ulysses Press, 2015)
- *The Survival Medicine Handbook,* by Joseph Alton and Amy Alton, 4th ed. (Doom and Bloom, 2021)
- *PDR for Herbal Medicines,* by Thomson Healthcare, 4th ed. (Thomson Reuters, 2007)
- *Where There Is No Doctor,* by David Werner, Carol Thuman, and Jane Maxwell, 2nd ed. (Hesperian Health Guides, 2024)
- *Where There Is No Dentist,* by Murray Dickson, 13th updated printing (Hesperian Foundation, 2010)

BUILDING TRADES

Basic information on carpentry, plumbing, and electrical systems can be useful. There's no way to tell right now what will happen down the road and what utilities may still be running for some time. Either way, you can't count on your local handyman to be available to take care of repairs when the need arises. Home Depot has published some very good books on these subjects, as has Black and Decker.

WILDERNESS SURVIVAL SKILLS

Many wilderness skills will be helpful around the homestead. Having reference materials to use for brushing up your skills will be welcome. There are many quality books on this subject, including manuals issued by the Boy Scouts. Other recommendations include the following:

- *Stay Alive! Survival Skills You Need*, by John D. McCann (Krause Publications, 2011)
- *Extreme Wilderness Survival*, by Craig Caudill (Page Street Publishing, 2017)
- *101 Skills You Need to Survive in the Woods*, by Kevin Estela (Page Street Publishing, 2019)

FICTION AND ENTERTAINMENT

Even if you personally don't enjoy recreational reading, there may very well be others in your group who will appreciate that you stocked up on books to pass the time. Novels, including the classics as well as contemporary works, and short story anthologies will be welcome. You can also include books on creating your own games, crafts, and other fun stuff to do.

WHERE TO GET YOUR BOOKS

Where to look for books for your home library? You can order almost anything you can imagine from online retailers like Amazon, but even their discounted prices can put a large ding in your wallet. Check out your local library for book sales during the year. Rummage sales and thrift stores are also great places to stock up on books inexpensively.

Many if not most preppers have also amassed tons of documents they've downloaded from the internet: PDFs, emails, all sorts of great stuff. Keep in mind that you may not be able to access all that information if the power goes out and/or your computer gets fried. Take the time now to print out that stuff and organize it in binders.

WEEK 49 ASSIGNMENTS

TASKS

☐ Inventory your current library and determine the areas in which you're lacking reference materials.

☐ Begin putting together a wish list of specific books you'd like to acquire as well as topics you'd like to get books about. Use Google and Amazon to find titles and other information. What I've done in the past is use Amazon's Wish List feature to keep a list of books I'm searching for, then take that list with me when I'm out book shopping.

☐ Make plans to visit local rummage sales regularly during this spring and summer. Take the time to stop at local thrift stores periodically to check their shelves. You can often find some great stuff for literally pennies on the dollar. Inquire at your area libraries, too, about their upcoming book sales.

SAVINGS

☐ Add $10 to your Prepper Savings Account.

Total Prepper Savings Account: [   ]

WATER STORAGE

☐ Store 1 gallon (or two 2-liter bottles) of water per person or a case of bottled water for the household.

Total Water Storage: [   ]

GROCERY LIST

☐ 3 cans vegetables, your choice
☐ 2 cans fruit, your choice, but stick with those packed in water or juice, rather than syrup
☐ 1 treat, such as a bag of hard candy or a canister of hot cocoa mix (the type that mixes with water, not milk)
☐ 1 can chili or stew, your choice
☐ 1 package or jar gravy, your choice
☐ 1 box powdered milk
☐ 1 pound white rice

☐ **WEEK COMPLETED**

Date:_____

WEEK 50
EMERGENCY LIGHTING

This week, I want to talk about lighting. It's important, even critical, to be able to see what you're doing, and in a grid-down situation, that can be difficult without planning ahead.

Of course, there are many ways to provide artificial light inside a home or retreat. Candles are inexpensive, especially if you pick them up at after-Christmas sales. It really doesn't matter if it's the middle of August and you're burning candles with Santa and reindeer on the sides. Light is light, right? The downside of candles is that they can be a safety hazard. *Never* leave a lit flame unattended. Be sure every candle you light is on a stable surface, so there's no risk of it toppling over. Also, candles don't last forever. A lot depends on the actual composition of the candle, of course, but don't look to candles for your primary backup light source in a power outage.

Oil lamps, sometimes called hurricane lamps, are a step up from candles. They last longer and burn cleaner. Glass ones are fragile, though, so again caution is warranted. If you go this route, be sure to stock up on plenty of lamp oil. Bear in mind that when you blow them out, the glass can get very sooty, so you'll need to clean them regularly.

Battery-powered flashlights are great for portable light. Buy LED ones rather than incandescent. LEDs will be brighter and last longer, in terms of both battery life and bulb life. There are many varieties of crank-powered flashlights as well, some better than others. You pretty much get what you pay for. If you pick up a few at the dollar store, don't expect them to last as long, or be as bright, as the ones you buy at a sporting goods store. I'm admittedly something of a flashlight junkie and have them scattered throughout the house as well as in almost all my kits.

Headlamps have come a long way and are highly recommended. The old kind that used incandescent bulbs was often hot, heavy, and uncomfortable. Today's headlamps use LED bulbs and are both lightweight and bright. Headlamps are excellent for when you need both hands free. They're not overly expensive either, if you shop around.

Handheld spotlights are useful but have limited battery life. Most of the ones I've seen lately charge an internal battery via an AC adapter or a 12-volt car adapter. They do give off a ton of light, which can be handy, but if the grid is down, you might have trouble keeping them charged.

Solar lights, the kind used in landscape projects, can be great to have. They're fairly cheap and give off enough light to read by, if you keep the light close by. Set them outside to charge during the day, then bring them in at night. Not a perfect solution by any means, but given that many people already have these lining their front walks, it's simple enough to bring them in after sundown.

WEEK 50 ASSIGNMENTS

TASKS

☐ Go through your lists and then check the house again and see what you already have on hand for emergency lighting. Purchase new batteries as needed, but I strongly advise you to consider using crank- and solar-powered lights.

☐ Take a look back through past assignments and see what you've missed. Plug the holes as you can.

SAVINGS

☐ Add $10 to your Prepper Savings Account.

Total Prepper Savings Account: ☐

WATER STORAGE

☐ Store 1 gallon (or two 2-liter bottles) of water per person or a case of bottled water for the household.

Total Water Storage: ☐

GROCERY LIST

☐ 3 cans vegetables, your choice

☐ 2 cans fruit, your choice, but stick with those packed in water or juice, rather than syrup

☐ 2 cans meat (tuna, chicken, beef), your choice

☐ 2 cans soup, not condensed (they require water)

☐ 1 box granola bars, protein bars, or equivalent

☐ 1 package nuts, dried fruit, or trail mix

☐ 1 pound dry beans, your choice

☐ **WEEK COMPLETED**

Date:_____

WEEK 51
DRILLS, DRILLS, AND MORE DRILLS

You should have plans in place for different scenarios, such as the ones below:

- Emergency evacuation from your home
- Lengthy power outage because of weather or other causes
- Stranded at home for several days or more

All the planning in the world, though, isn't going to help much if you don't do test runs. It's true that practice makes perfect. By running through your plans in real time, you'll likely discover holes or gaps in your preparation. It's vastly better to find those problems now, while you have time to address them, rather than when you're doing it for real.

This week, I want you to pick at least one realistic scenario and play it out as a drill or exercise. Make it as real as you can while still being safe. For example, if you choose to drill for a lengthy power outage, turn off your circuit breakers for a day or two. You may want to leave the ones on for your fridge and freezer, and just pretend they aren't working. There's little sense in letting food go to waste just for the sake of the exercise.

If you're doing an evacuation, make it a surprise for the family to get their blood pumping. Give everyone a short period of time to follow the plan for getting out of the house.

Just as important as the practice is the postdrill evaluation. Sit down with everyone and go over how it went. What worked and what didn't? What needs to change? Did everyone remember their responsibilities?

Be sure to ask for input from each family member. Sometimes we, the planners and leaders (so to speak), forget this important element to planning. We get so caught up in what we already know and want to share that we forget to see things from other perspectives.

Even if you're the only one in your home, you can still learn a thing or two when you do exercises like these. You may find out that you overlooked a key element in your planning.

Yes, drills are a pain in the arse for most of us. It throws us off our normal schedules and interrupts our daily lives.

But, then again, so do disasters.

WEEK 51 ASSIGNMENTS

TASKS

☐ Do one or more drills, as discussed above. Be sure to sit down with everyone and recap how the drills went and identify areas for improvement.

SAVINGS

☐ Add $15 to your Prepper Savings Account.

Total Prepper Savings Account: ☐

WATER STORAGE

☐ Store 1 gallon (or two 2-liter bottles) of water per person or a case of bottled water for the household.

Total Water Storage: ☐

GROCERY LIST

☐ 3 cans vegetables, your choice

☐ 2 cans fruit, your choice, but stick with those packed in water or juice, rather than syrup

☐ 1 can chili or stew, your choice

☐ 1 package or jar gravy, your choice

☐ 1 pound pasta, your choice

☐ **WEEK COMPLETED**

Date:_____

WEEK 52

ELECTRICAL POWER

For most of us, electricity might seem to be a necessity, but it really is still a luxury. Sure, during an extended outage, we may feel as though we're experiencing some serious withdrawal symptoms from not being able to access our email, but we'll survive without it. That said, those outages can be made a bit more comfortable if we can at least turn on a fan and maybe a lamp or two.

To provide for our own electricity, most of us will need to turn to some sort of generator, either gas or solar powered. That, of course, begs the question of how large of a generator do we truly need?

The answer is going to be different for everyone. You'll need to do a bit of homework. Go through your house and decide what appliances and such you feel you would truly need running during a power outage. Let's make this easy. Grab a pen and notepad and visit each room of your house, jotting down every single thing that's plugged into an outlet. Don't forget the sump pump in the basement as well as all the kitchen appliances. Next to each item, write down the watt consumption, which is usually found either on a tag on the power cord or on a label on the item itself.

After you've gone through every room, sit down with the list and begin crossing off those things that are unnecessary for survival. Things like toasters and clock radios are likely among those items. Keep narrowing down the list until you're left with only those things that are vitally important.

Now, add up the watt consumption for your new list. This will give you an estimate of how large the generator will need to be to provide power for everything. I'm betting that once you start pricing out generators, you'll find a way to cross more items off that list, too. There's a little bit of wiggle room here. Not every single thing on the list will necessarily need to be running at the same time. The refrigerator may currently run about every other hour, but you could dial that down to every couple of hours and still keep the contents cool and safe, provided you can keep the teenager from opening the fridge door every ten minutes.

Lamps and other lights need power only at night. The sump pump needs to run only when there's water to be removed. TVs and DVD players won't be on constantly. So you can play the numbers game, at least a bit, and fudge on your needs when shopping.

There are two primary types of generators—gas and solar powered. Each has pros and cons. The gas generators are powerful and very easy to use. Start them up, plug in the extension cords or throw the transfer switch, and you're good to go. But they're also very noisy, similar to a gas lawn mower. As a result, it's tough to convince folks that you don't have one once you've started it up. They also require the use of fuel, sometimes quite a bit of it. Some of the popular brand names of gas generators include Generac and Westinghouse. They come in a wide range of sizes, from small enough to wheel around the backyard to "whole home" models permanently installed alongside the house.

There are also a couple of different configurations to gas-powered generators. The smaller models are designed to have a couple of extension cords plugged into them that you can run to where the power is needed. Larger ones will utilize a transfer switch that's installed in the side of your home. This switch runs to the electrical hookup inside the home and allows the home owner to switch household power from the utility company to the generator. This installation is not typically a DIY project but something that should be handled by a professional. An electrician will route certain circuits in the home in such a way that when the transfer switch is thrown, those circuits will get their power from the generator. Then when power is restored, they're switched back.

Solar-powered generators are another option. They're generally more expensive than their gas-powered counterparts. But they have some advantages. First, they're silent, given that there's no motor running inside. No fuel consumption, either. They soak up the sun's rays and store the power inside batteries, which provide the juice for your toys and whatnot. Jackery and Bluetti are two companies at the forefront of this technology.

One other option is to use portable solar panels for limited power. You won't be able to keep a refrigerator running with these, but you can charge cell phones and tablets quite easily, which might be all you truly need for limited outages.

WEEK 52 ASSIGNMENTS

TASKS

☐ Research, inventory, and prioritize all the power-consuming items in your home.

☐ Begin shopping around for generators, basing your selection on the power needs that you've calculated.

SAVINGS

☐ Add $15 to your Prepper Savings Account.

Total Prepper Savings Account: ☐

WATER STORAGE

☐ Store 1 gallon (or two 2-liter bottles) of water per person or a case of bottled water for the household.

Total Water Storage: ☐

GROCERY LIST

☐ 3 cans vegetables, your choice

☐ 2 cans fruit, your choice, but stick with those packed in water or juice, rather than syrup

☐ 2 cans meat (tuna, chicken, beef), your choice

☐ 2 cans soup, not condensed (they require water)

☐ 1 box (12 packages) ramen noodles

☐ 1 pound white rice

☐ **WEEK COMPLETED**

Date:_____

HOW DID YOU DO?

Assuming that you're not someone who skips to the last chapter to see how the story ends, pat yourself on the back for a job well done in completing the Countdown to Preparedness! I warned you at the outset that you were in for a workout, and you should feel very proud of yourself for making it to the end. Bravo!

If you've managed to purchase every item in the grocery lists in each lesson, here's what you should have on hand right now:

Type of Food	Expected Amount	Your Amount
Canned vegetables	156 cans	
Canned fruit	104 cans	
Canned meat	52 cans	
Canned soup	52 cans	
Oatmeal	6 canisters or boxes	
Canned chili or stew	25 cans	
Gravy	25 packages or jars	
Peanut butter	5 jars	
Granola or protein bars	11 boxes	
Jelly or fruit preserves	5 jars	

Type of Food	Expected Amount	Your Amount
Pasta sauce	10 jars	
Salt	3 canisters	
Baking mix	5 boxes	
Ramen noodles	11 boxes (132 packages)	
White rice	17 pounds	
Instant coffee	5 jars	
Dry soup mix	10 packages	
Cornmeal	3 bags	
Tea	5 boxes	
Dry beans	14 pounds	
Crackers	5 boxes	
Pasta	15 pounds	
Powdered milk	5 boxes	
Instant potatoes	2 boxes	
Flour	10 pounds	
Sugar	8 pounds	
Multivitamins	2 bottles	
Honey	2 jars	
Flavored drink mix	3 canisters	
Cooking oil	4 gallons	
Nuts, dried fruit, or trail mix	3 packages	

Don't forget several different types of treats for desserts and to help keep up morale!

The above should be plenty of food to keep an average family of four alive for several weeks without needing additional supplies. Coupled with garden produce, hunting, trapping, and/or fishing, this food pantry would go even further.

As for water, if you've set aside the amounts prescribed each and every week, rotating and replacing as needed, you should have at least 52 gallons of water set aside for each person, possibly even more if you've substituted cases of bottled water here and there. At a gallon of water per person per day, that's enough to last almost two months. Add in what you can drain from your water heater (say, an average of 30 gallons), as well as collected rainwater or melted ice and snow, and you should be able to stretch the water supply to three months or so.

Let's look at the Prepper Savings Account. Now, odds are good that you weren't able to contribute the specified amount every single week. And if you've been using this account as you should, dipping into it when you find needed supplies at great prices, you aren't going to have much money left. All told, ideally you've contributed almost $700 to your account. That's a large chunk of change that you can use to buy prepping supplies. But the hidden bonus is that you've developed a habit of coming up with an extra $10–$20 each week to set aside. That's one habit that you want to stick with for quite some time to come.

Speaking of going forward, don't stop now. Keep adding to your food and water storage as well as learning new prepping skills. While you should take a well-deserved break after completing the Countdown to Preparedness, you should also recognize that prepping is truly a lifestyle, and there's no definite end point. Keep on keepin' on!

ONE FINAL LESSON: WHEN NORMALCY RETURNS

Something that's often missing in discussions about prepping is what happens after the crisis has passed. It's important to recognize that the vast majority of disasters aren't going to be societal collapse situations. While it might be chaos for a time, at some point order will be restored. When that happens, there may be some pushback or consequences for actions that were taken.

The neighbors you thumbed your nose at when they were pleading with you for help? They managed to make it through the bad times and are still residing next door. That might not be a fun conversation when you both happen to be rolling your garbage cans out to the road at the same time.

That house you raided for food and supplies when the owners seemed to be gone? They've returned and would really like to speak with you about the damage to their back door as well as the several rifles that appear to be missing. That conversation may involve some folks wearing badges.

If you have local family or friends who are aware you prep, there's a very good chance they may show up asking for your help in a crisis. You can be as hard-nosed as you want in conversations with them, but if they feel they have nowhere else to turn, they're going to knock on your door. The way I see it, you basically have three options:

1. Plan to turn them away, by force if necessary.
2. Plan to prep for them. Add extras to your own supplies to account for their needs.
3. Plan to not be there when they arrive, which may or may not be feasible.

Forcing a stranger off the porch, possibly with the assistance of a handgun or rifle, is one thing. Doing it to Uncle Frank and his family, folks with whom you've broken bread every Christmas for the last two decades, is another thing altogether. And if push comes to shove, how far are you willing to go?

All too often, prepping discussions seem to end at about the same time they would in a disaster novel, with little or no talk about what happens next. While desperate times might call for desperate measures, bear in mind that at some point you may be called upon to answer for those measures taken. Maybe don't be so eager to engage in behavior that could prove problematic down the road. Plan ahead so your actions are reasonable and appropriate, rather than forced by a lack of other options. That's sort of the whole point of prepping, isn't it?

INDEX

A
acetaminophen (Tylenol), 61
adhesive bandages, 11
alarms, 150–152
    DIY approach, 151
    motion lights, 151
    remotely monitored, 151
    Wi-Fi-enabled cameras, 151
allergic emergencies (anaphylaxis), 62
aspirin, 61
assignments, weekly. *See specific weeks*
asthma, 62–63

B
baby wipes, 138
baking essentials, 108
baking staples, 181
bank accounts, 174
Baofeng, 115
baseline, 156
basic supplies, wound, 59–60
basic water storage, 18–22
battery-powered flashlights, 193
Benadryl, 61
Betty Crocker cookbooks, 108
bills, 174
blades for survival, 121–124
    110 Folding Hunter from Buck Knives, 122
    Cold Steel Kukri, 122
    EXT-1 from Bark River Knives, 122
    Field Scalpel from D. Tope Knives, 122
    folding knives, 122
    Grunt 2.0 from Vehement Knives, 122
    Huntsman from Edge Knife Works, 122
    Livewire from Kershaw Knives, 122
    machete-type blade, 121
    Model 1 from White River Knives, 122
    Mongrel from Vehement Knives, 122
    Mudbug from Smith & Sons Knives, 122
    pocket-carry fixed-blade knives, 122
    pocketknife, 121
    Republic from Cold Steel, 122
    sheath knife, 121
    South Pole from TRC Knives, 122
    Swiss Army Knife, 122
    Ursus 45 from White River Knives, 122
bleach, 51–52
boiling water, 51
bug out bags, 28–31
building trades, 190
bungee cords, 166
butterfly bandages, 60

C

camp stoves, 97
campfires, 97
canned vegetables, 181
carbon monoxide (CO) detectors, 118
casement windows, 148
claritin dissolving tabs (loratadine), 61
Clayton, Bruce, 46
cleaning products, 138
cleanliness, 70–72
Cold Steel Kukri, 122
collar and id tags
   for pets, 43
communications, 64–66
   cell phones, 64–66
   person-to-person communication, 65
   two-way radios, 64–66
contacts, 174
coolers, 167
Cooper Color Code, 157
Condition Orange, 157
Condition Red, 157
Condition White, 157
Condition Yellow, 157
Cooper, Jeff, 157
Countdown to Preparedness, 2
crank radios, 140–142

D

death file, 25–27, 173–176
   bank accounts, 174
   bills, 174
   contacts, 174
   insurance policies, 174
   last words, 175
   legal documents, 173
   online accounts, 174
   real estate, 174
   safes, 174
debris hut, 178
debt reduction, 23–24
decorative firepits, 97
defense weapon, 126
diabetes, 62
diapers/diaper cream, 138
diphenhydramine (Benadryl), 61
doors, 146–147
double-hung windows, 148
drills, 196–198
duct tape, 128, 166

E

education, 39–40
elastic bandages, 60
electrical power, 199–202
   generators, 200
emergency lighting, 193–195
   battery-powered flashlights, 193
   handheld spotlights, 194
   headlamps, 194
   hurricane lamps, 193
   oil lamps, 193
   solar lights, 194
emergency savings, 24
entertainment, 39, 85–87
equipment. *See* safety equipment
everyday carry, 126–129
   defense weapon, 126
   duct tape, 128
   extra cash, 128
   fire kit, 127
   first aid, 127
   knife, 126
   lighter, 126
   magnifying glass, 128
   off-body EDC bag, 127
   on-body gear, 126
   pocket flashlight, 126
   power bank and cords, 127
   tool kit, 127
   tourniquet, 126
   tweezers, 128
extra cash, 128

F

Family Radio Service (FRS), 65
fiction and entertainment, 190
financial preps, 23–27
firearms maintenance, 188

firearms, 90–92
　12-gauge shotgun, 90
　handgun, 91
　hunting rifle, 90
　long rifle (LR), 90
first aid and medical care, for pets, 43
first aid supplies and training, 59–63
　basic supplies, wound, 59–60
　butterfly bandages, 60
　elastic bandages, 60
　general medications, 61
　roller gauze, 60
　special needs considerations, 62–63
　spray bottle of normal saline, 60
　sterile cotton swabs, 60
　sterile gauze, 60
　vinyl medical gloves, 61
first aid/medical supplies, 11–12
folding knives, 122
food, for pets, 43
food off-grid, preparing, 96–98
　camp stoves, 97
　campfires, 97
　decorative firepits, 97
　grills, 96
　solar ovens, 97
food storage, 10–11, 46–48
　basic food storage, 46–48
　and preservation, 188
　rice, 47

G

garbage bags, 138
garden planning, 55–58
　square-foot gardening, 56
gas powered generators, 200
12-gauge shotgun, 90
General Mobile Radio Service (GMRS), 65
glucagon injection, 62
glucometer, 62
grills, 96

H

ham radio, 114–116
　shortwave, 115
hand sanitizer, 138
hand tools, 103–107
　baking essentials, 108
　basic tools, 103
　bow saw, 103
　channel lock pliers, 103
　crowbar, 104
　duct tape, 103
　electrical tape, 103
　extendable magnet, 104
　hacksaw, 104
　hammer, 103
　herbs and spices, 108
　intermediate-level tools, 104–105
　loppers, 104
　needle-nose pliers, 104
　pry bar, 103
　screwdriver set, 103
　sledgehammer, 104
　socket set, 104
　WD-40 or equivalent, 103
　wire cutters, 103
　wrenches, 103
handgun, 91
handheld spotlights, 194
headlamps, 194
herbs and spices, 108
hidden storage, 100–102
　basement ceiling, 100
　ventilation ducts, 100
homesteading skills, 187
human waste disposal, 67–69
　alternatives to toilet paper, 68
　burning, 68
hunting rifle, 90
hurricane lamps, 193
hydrogen peroxide, 11
hygiene, 12, 39

I

ibuprofen, 61
immediate family, attending to, 32–34
Imodium A-D, 61
improvised weapons, 111–113
    pepper spray works, 112
    Tasers, 112
individual retirement accounts (IRAs), 25
Insulin pump supplies, 62
insurance policies, 174
intermediate-level hand tools, 104–105
inventory, the basics, 184–186
Ipecac bottle, 61

K

ketodiastix, 62
knife, 126
Krehbiel, Jane-Alexandra, 59

L

legal documents, 173
lighter, 126
lighting, emergency. See emergency lighting
lists, 10–14
    first aid/medical supplies, 11–12
    food storage, 10–11
    hygiene, 12
    miscellaneous, 13
    tools, 12
    water storage, 11
long rifle (LR), 90
loratadine, 61

M

machete-type blade, 121
magnifying glass, 128
making fire, 82–84
manual can openers, 167
mass-casualty events, 130–133
medical and dental issues, 76–78
microclimates, building, 177–180
    debris hut, 178
month 1 totals, 27
    week 1, lists, 14
    week 2, out with the old, 15–17
    week 3, basic water storage, 18–22
    week 4, financial preps, 23–27

N

National Oceanic and Atmospheric Administration (NOAA), 141
nebulizer treatments, 62
networking, 79–81
    barter/trade, 79–80
    pooling of resources, 79
    security, 80
    sounding boards, 79
nonfood pantry items, 137–139
    baby wipes, 138
    cleaning products, 138
    diapers, diaper cream, and crib bedding, 138
    garbage bags, 138
    hand sanitizer, 138
    paper plates, cups, and bowls, 137
    paper towels, 137
    toilet paper, 138
nutrition, 38–41

O

odds and ends to stock up on, 166
    bungee cords, 166
    coolers, 167
    duct tape, 166
    manual can openers, 167
    paracord, 166
    plywood and dimensional lumber, 166
    sewing materials, 166
    tarps, 166
    trash bags, 167
off-body EDC bag, 127
oil lamps, 193
Omeprazole, 61
on-body gear, 126

online accounts, 174
operations security (OPSEC), 40
outbuildings, 148–149
over-the-counter medications, 11, 73–75

P

pantry, bulking up, 181–183
   baking staples, 181
   canned vegetables, 181
paper plates/cups/bowls, 137
paper towels, 137
paracord, 166
pepper spray works, 112
Pepto-Bismol, 61
pets, in prep considerations, 42–45
   carrier, 43
   collar and id tags, 43
   first aid and medical care, 43
   food, 43
   pet carrier, 43
   recent photo of you and your pet, 43
   sanitation, 44
   water, 42
planning to regroup, 134–136
plywood, 166
pocket flashlight, 126
pocketknife, 121
police scanners, 140–142
pool shock, 51
postcollapse excursions, 162–165
power devices. *See* battery-powered flashlights; electrical power; everyday carry; gas powered generators; solar powered generators
practicing situational awareness, 156–159
Prepper's Complete Book of Disaster Readiness, The, 1
Prepper's Home Defense, 1
Prepper's Long-Term Survival Guide, 2
prepping
   talking to your immediate family about, 32–34

prescription medications, 73–75
Primary, Alternate, Contingency, and Emergency (PACE) planning, 35–37
   Alternate, 35–36
   Contingency, 35–36
   Emergency, 35–36
   Primary, 35–36

R

real estate, 174
reducing footprint, 153–155
retirement planning, 25
Riegert, Keith, 2
roller gauze, 60
Rubber tourniquet, 61

S

safes, 174
safety equipment, 117–120
   flashlight, 118
   masks, 118
   PASS, 118
sanitation, for pets, 44
security and defense, 188
sewing materials, 166
sheath knife, 121
single side band (SSB), 115
site security survey, 143–145
sliding windows, 148
solar lights, 194
solar ovens, 97
solar powered generators, 200–201
special needs considerations, 62–63
   allergic emergencies (anaphylaxis), 62
   asthma, 62–63
   diabetes, 62
special prep considerations, children, 38–41
   education, 39–40
   entertainment, 39
   hygiene, 39
   nutrition, 38–41
special prep considerations, pets, 42–45. *See also* pets, in prep considerations

spray bottle of normal saline, 60
square-foot gardening, 56
sterile cotton swabs, 60
sterile gauze, 60
storage. *See* basic water storage; food storage; hidden storage; odds and ends to stock up on
straw filters, 52–53
sugar, spice, and everything nice, 107–110
survival and preparedness library, 187–192. *See also* blades for survival
    building trades, 190
    fiction and entertainment, 190
    firearms maintenance, 188
    food storage and preservation, 188
    homesteading skills, 187
    medical, 189
    security and defense, 188
    wild edibles and medicinals, 189
    wilderness survival skills, 190
Swiss Army Knife, 122

T

tarps, 166
toilet paper, 138
tools. *See* hand tools
tourniquet, 126
transportation, alternate modes of, 93–95
    motorcycles, 94
trash bags, 167
tweezers, 128
Tylenol, 61

V

vehicle emergency kits, 169–172
vinyl medical gloves, 61

W

water
    for pets, 42
    storage, 11
    water-purification tablets, 52

water filtration and purification, 50–54
    bleach, 51–52
    boiling water, 51
    straw filters, 52–53
    water bottles, 53
    water-purification tablets, 52
WaterBOB, 20
week 1, 10–14
    assignments, 14
    lists, 10–13
week 2, 15–17
    assignments, 17
    out with the old, 15–17
week 3, 18–22
    assignments, 22
    basic water storage, 18–22
    water needs, calculation, 18–20
    water storage, 20–21
week 4, 23–27
    assignments, 26
    debt reduction, 23–24
    emergency savings, 24
    financial preps, 23–27
week 5, 28–31
    assignments, 30–31
    bug out bags, 28–31
week 6, 32–34
    assignments, 34
    talking to your immediate family about prepping, 32–34
week 7, 35–37
    assignments, 37
    pace planning, 35–37. *See also* Primary, Alternate, Contingency, and Emergency (PACE) planning
week 8, 38–41
    assignments, 41
    special prep considerations, children, 38–41
week 9, 42–45
    assignments, 45
    special prep considerations, pets, 42–45

week 10, 46–48
    assignments, 48
    basic food storage, 46–48
week 11, 50–54
    assignments, 54, 72
    water filtration and purification, 50–54
week 12, 55–58
    assignments, 58
    planning garden, 55–58
week 13, 59–63
    assignments, 63
    basic first aid supplies and training, 59–63
week 14, 64–66
    assignments, 66
    communications, two-way radios and cell phones, 64–66
week 15, 67–69
    assignments, 69
    human waste disposal, 67–69
week 16, 70–72
    assignments, 72
    keeping clean, 70–72
week 17, 73–75
    assignments, 75
    over-the-counter and prescription medications, 73–75
week 18, 76–78
    assignments, 78
    medical and dental issues, 76–78
week 19, 79-81
    assignments, 81
    networking, 79–81
week 20, 82–84
    assignments, 84
    making fire, 82–84
week 21, 85–87
    assignments, 87
    entertainment, 85–87
week 22, 90–92
    assignments, 92
    firearms, 90–92

week 23, 93–95
    alternate modes of transportation, 93–95
    assignments, 95
week 24, 96–99
    assignments, 99
    preparing food off-grid, 96–98
week 25, 100–102
    assignments, 102
    hidden storage, 100–102
week 26, 103–106
    assignments, 106
    hand tools, 103–107
week 27, 107–110
    assignments, 110
    sugar, spice, and everything nice, 107–110
week 28, 111–113
    assignments, 113
    improvised weapons, 111–113
week 29, 114–116
    assignments, 116
    ham radio, 114–116
week 30, 117–120
    assignments, 120
    safety equipment, 117–120
week 31, 121–124
    assignments, 124
    blades for survival, 121–124
week 32, 126–129
    assignments, 129
    everyday carry, 126–129
week 33, 130–133
    assignments, 133
    mass-casualty events, 130–133
week 34, 134–136
    assignments, 136
    planning to regroup, 134–136
week 35, 137–139
    assignments, 139
    nonfood pantry items, 137–139

week 36, 140–142
    assignments, 142
    crank radios and police scanners, 140–142
week 37, 143–145
    assignments, 145
    site security survey, 143–145
week 38, 146–149
    assignments, 149
    doors, 146–147
    outbuildings, 148–149
    structure hardening, 146–149
    windows, 147–148
week 39, 150–152
    assignments, 152
    structure hardening, 150–152
week 40, 153–155
    assignments, 155
    reducing your footprint, 153–155
week 41, 156–159
    assignments, 159
    practicing situational awareness, 156–159
week 42, 162–165
    assignments, 165
    planning for postcollapse excursions, 162–165
week 43, 166–168
    assignments, 168
    odds and ends to stock up on, 166
week 44, 169–172
    assignments, 172
    vehicle emergency kits, 169–172
week 45, 173–176
    assignments, 176
    death file, 173–176
week 46, 177–180
    assignments, 180
    building microclimates, 177–180
week 47, 181–183
    assignments, 183
    bulking up the pantry, 181–183
week 48, 184–186
    assignments, 186
    inventory, 184–186
week 49, 187–192
    assignments, 192
    survival and preparedness library, 187–192
week 50, 193–195
    assignments, 195
    emergency lighting, 193–195
week 51, 196–198
    assignments, 198
    drills, 196–198
week 52, 199–202
    assignments, 202
    electrical power, 199–202
    "whole home" models, 200
wild edibles and medicinals, 189
wilderness survival skills, 190
windows, 147–148
    casement windows, 148
    double-hung windows, 148
    sliding windows, 148
wire splint, 61

ACKNOWLEDGMENTS

First and always, to my wife, Tammy, thank you for giving me that swift kick in the ass all those years ago. It was very much needed and very much appreciated.

To Chris Golden, my mentor and friend, thank you for always being there with advice and support.

To Brian Keene, my other mentor and friend, thank you for always looking out for me.

Special thanks to Craig Caudill for writing the foreword. Thank you for your friendship as well as your keen insights.

To the team at Ulysses Press, an author couldn't dream of better folks to team with, that's for sure. Thank you for everything.

And finally, to my readers. Thank you for allowing me to take up some space in your head from time to time.

ABOUT THE AUTHOR

Jim Cobb is a recognized authority on disaster readiness and related topics. He is the editor in chief of *Backwoods Survival Guide* magazine. He's authored more than ten books, including *Prepper's Home Defense* and *The Prepper's Complete Book of Disaster Readiness*. He is also a cohost on the *How to Survive 2025* podcast. Jim has been involved with emergency preparedness in one capacity or another for almost four decades. He and his wife have three adult sons and a houseful of assorted critters. You can find Jim online on Facebook @jim.cobb.739 or email him directly at jim@survivalweekly.com.